TOM LACALAMITA

ALSO BY TOM LACALAMITA

The Ultimate Bread Machine Cookbook

The Ultimate Pasta Machine Cookbook

The Ultimate Espresso Machine Cookbook

THE ULTIMATE PRESSURE COOKER COOKBOOK

RECIPES FROM THE MEDITERRANEAN TRADITION

PHOTOGRAPHS BY ILISA KATZ

FOOD STYLIST: ROSCOE BETSILL

PROP STYLIST: EDWARD KEMPER DESIGN

ILLUSTRATIONS BY LAURIE DAVIS

SIMON & SCHUSTER

SIMON & SCHUSTER
Rockefeller Center
1230 Avenue of the Americas
New York, NY 10020

Designed by Elina Nudelman
Illustrations by Laurie Davis

Manufactured in the United States of America

3   5   7   9   10   8   6   4   2

Library of Congress Cataloging-in-Publication Data
Lacalamita, Tom.
The ultimate pressure cooker cookbook : recipes from the Mediterranean tradition /
Tom Lacalamita ; photographs by Ilisa Katz ; food stylist, Roscoe Betsill ; prop stylist,
Edward Kemper Design; illustrations by Laurie Davis.
        p.   cm.
        Includes index.
        1. Pressure cookery.   2. Cookery, Mediterranean.   I. Title.
                TX840.P7L33   1997
        641.5'87—dc21   96-40229
                        CIP
                ISBN 0-684-82496-5

For Yayi and Cristina

ACKNOWLEDGMENTS

Thanks go to my editor, Gillian Casey Sowell, for the opportunity to do this book and her guidance and unending support, and to the rest of the Simon & Schuster team: Jim Thiel, Amy Hill, and Toni Rachiele, for their respective contributions along the path of this book's development.

Also to Ilisa Katz and Roscoe Betsill, for their beautiful portrayal of the food on film, and to prop stylist Edward Kemper Design. Thanks also to Laurie Davis, for the skillful illustrations.

Sincere thanks to my special friend Glenna Vance, for sharing with me her encounter with a pressure cooker as a child in the late 1940s, and for the nutritional analyses, enthusiasm, and support.

A special mention to my mother-in-law, Mercedes Ruiz, one of the best Spanish cooks and bakers that I know, for sharing with me many of the wonderful Spanish farmhouse recipes she has prepared over the years for our family.

My sincere appreciation goes to all the manufacturers credited on page 195 for providing the equipment and technical information needed in developing this book.

And most important, thanks to my family and friends, for sharing with me my love of food and for the knowledge and skills they have so graciously provided me over the years.

CONTENTS

PART ONE

INTRODUCTION

PRESSURE COOKERS: DISPELLING THE MISCONCEPTIONS

Pressure cookers have unfortunately been the subject of numerous horror stories and the butt of jokes on television sitcoms or even television commercials. Never has there been a kitchen product that stirs up so much fear and suspicion. Mostly because of stories like this one told to me by my friend Glenna Vance about an evening in the late 1940s:

> *At the end of the summer Mom had gone shopping in Erie with her friend, Alma, and Dad and I had decided to cook dinner. With plenty of vegetables from the garden, a freezer full of beef, and a new pressure cooker, it seemed like a good idea. We loaded the pressure cooker full to the top and placed it on the hot burner. Soon the jiggler valve started to rock and twirl. Dad had never seen it do that before, so he put a heavy, clear ashtray on top of it to steady it. The ashtray fit perfectly over the valve and it seemed to do the trick. While dinner was cooking, I was busy cutting up peaches for dessert when the next thing I knew we were under attack. The ashtray flew through the air along with the jiggler valve and the rubber pressure plug. Steam was shooting out of the pressure cooker so high that it hit the ceiling. I never saw Dad move so fast in my life. He pulled the pressure cooker off the burner and twisted off the lid. Before we knew it, bits of meat and vegetables were dripping off the ceiling.*

If Glenna had told me that these events had taken place recently using one of the new pressure cookers available today, I would have never believed her, since the design and safety features found on today's pots essentially eliminate this sort of problem.

Today's pressure cookers are manufactured by reputable cookware companies who have invested years of experience, research and development, and reputation in their product, while incorporating the latest technological advances. In fact, most pressure cookers sold today are Underwriter's Laboratory (UL) listed, demonstrating that the unit meets the minimum safety requirements of this independent safety-regulatory agency. Nevertheless, since the pressure cooker is a cooking utensil with specialized operating functions, there are a few basic practices, discussed in detail later in this chapter, that should be followed when using your pressure cooker in order to obtain the best results.

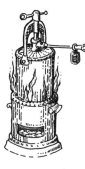

THE HISTORY OF PRESSURE COOKERS:
A EUROPEAN INVENTION

> *It was the need to cook which taught man to use fire, and it was by using fire that man conquered Nature.*
>
> —BRILLAT-SAVARIN

Since the days of early humans and the discovery of fire, we have been fascinated with finding new and faster ways of cooking and preserving food. The need to survive prompted prehistoric people to develop the most basic cooking methods. For modern people it has been curiosity about technology and the desire to apply it to everyday life that has led to improved cooking methods.

The seventeenth-century French inventor Denis Papin was one of those interested in developing a new method to cook food quickly at relatively low cost. In 1680, Papin introduced a revolutionary new cooking device, the *marmite de Papin,* or the Papin Digester. From what little we know, the Papin Digester was made from cast metal, perhaps iron, with a lid that locked in place with a screwlike clamping mechanism. As the food heated in its cooking liquid, the trapped steam raised the cooking temperature to at least 15 percent higher than the boiling point of water. This very hot steam cooked the food quicker than the ordinary methods available at that time. The only problem with this new technology was the lack of understanding about regulating the steam pressure and the inability to accurately regulate the cooking temperature, leading, unfortunately, to many an exploding digester. Another major drawback was the lack of technology to produce machine-stamped pots (made from a single piece of metal). The cast or molded pots that were used would eventually crack along their seams under high levels of pressure, spewing the contents sky-high. Even though Papin never saw his concept and invention reach its full potential, he at least provided the basic notion of cooking under high pressure.

It was not until the very late 1700s and the early 1800s, with France in the throes of revolution and Napoleon's armies on the move, that the general concept of Papin's digester would be embraced as a way to cook and preserve food quickly, with a reduced risk of contamination. The French government was faced with the daunting task of feeding its army, navy, and civilian population at a time when malnutrition was reaching epidemic proportions. In a desperate move, they offered a 12,000-franc reward to anyone who could develop a successful way of preserving food for later consumption. Nicholas Appert, a Parisian brewer turned confectioner, entered the competition and, in 1809, was awarded the prize money for his revolutionary techniques of preserving food under high pressure with steam.

Combining his experience as a brewer and confectioner, Appert hypothesized that certain ingredients, like sugar, act as a natural preservative, and that other ingredients encourage fermentation to take place, ultimately speeding up spoilage. Appert believed that by heating food at high temperatures in well-sealed, sterilized glass jars, the fermentation process or spoilage due to bacteria could be slowed down or eliminated without altering the flavor of the food. According to Appert, the way to effectively do this was to:

> First enclose the substances you wish to preserve in bottles or jars; second, close the openings of your vessels with the greatest care, for success depends principally on the seal; third, submit the substances, thus enclosed, to the action of boiling water in a bain-marie for a period of longer or shorter duration depending on their nature and the manner I shall indicate for each kind of foodstuff; fourth, remove the bottles from the bain-marie at the appropriate time.

At the time of Appert's work, the exact causes of food spoilage were unknown, and they would not be understood until almost a century later, with the work of Louis Pasteur. Nevertheless, Appert revived interest in the pressure method of cooking and preserving established by Papin by developing canning procedures for more than fifty different types of food. Without any formal scientific training, Appert determined by trial and error that when heat was applied to food sealed in a container impervious to air, it somehow prevented food from spoiling. Filling sterilized, wide-mouth jars with food and corking them securely, Appert introduced the concept of preserving food by vacuum sealing, a concept that led to the development of the canning industry in the early 1900s in both the United Kingdom and the United States. Since Appert did not bother to patent his process, preserving food in vacuum-sealed jars soon became popular with housewives on both sides of the Atlantic.

Appert's method was not foolproof, however, and occasionally preserves caused illness and death when the food was improperly processed. After Appert's death in 1841, his nephew, Raymond Chevallier-Appert, continued to work on his uncle's theories. He invented and patented a sterilizer that worked under high-pressure steam, providing more consistent results. This invention was the true forerunner of today's pressure cooker.

THE PRESSURE COOKER IN THE UNITED STATES

After serious outbreaks of food poisoning in the early 1900s, including the deaths of thirty-five people between 1919 and 1920 from botulism caused by improperly jarred olives, the United States Department of Agriculture officially announced that the only way to safely process low-acid foods was to use pressure canners. All commercial canneries were required to be equipped with pressure-canning equipment. One of the first companies to manufacture and sell fifty-gallon–capacity pressure canners was Northwestern Iron and Steel Works of Eau Claire, Wisconsin, founded in 1905. But fifty-gallon pressure canners were not useful for those who wanted to preserve food at home. In 1915, Presto, now known as National Presto Industries, developed and introduced a line of ten-gallon aluminum pressure canners for home use in order to meet the growing demand from American consumers who wanted a safer way to preserve food.

Early pressure canners were quite cumbersome. Even though they were made from molded aluminum, a material we associate with lightweight strength, they were large and heavy. Early models also required the user to screw and unscrew six to eight wing nuts on the lid to close and open the unit. Both Presto and others were inspired by the popularity of this device to try to develop a unit that was easier to use. In 1938, Alfred Vischer, after much trial and error, introduced his Flex-Seal Speed Cooker, the first saucepan-sized pressure cooker. Competition soon followed, with both Presto and Mirro also introducing saucepan-sized pressure cookers. Success would have to wait a few years longer, however, since America, just on the verge of entering World War II, was busy converting all civilian manufacturing facilities to war production. While this temporarily ended the manufacture of pressure cookers for consumer use, production of commercial pressure canners continued during this period in order to meet the growing need to feed GIs overseas.

By the late 1940s, with peace in Europe and the Pacific, the consumer pressure-cooker market took off. Almost overnight there were eleven different manufacturers offering eighty-five different pressure saucepans (as they were called). Prices dropped and quality suffered as unscrupulous manufacturers entered the market to capitalize on the growing demand. While consumers were well aware of the benefits of using a pressure cooker for preparing meals—cooking in just one-third of the time, preserving vitamin and mineral content of food, and saving both food flavor and color—they also grew more skeptical with the increasing number of horror stories about exploding and rupturing units. Little by little, companies began to drop out of the category, until finally only those truly dedicated to the development of safe, foolproof units, like Presto and Mirro, remained.

While pressure cookers revolutionized how the average homemaker was able to cook in the years following World War II, other advances in food preparation would soon begin to overshadow their convenience. With the advent of products like frozen entrées and prepared foods in the postwar years, America's eating habits began to change dramatically. Consumers were seeking an even higher level of convenience than that afforded by the pressure cooker, and it began to fall out of favor. It would not be until the late 1960s and early 1970s, which saw an increased awareness of healthy eating, that pressure cookers would begin to once again gain in popularity.

As we entered the 1990s, many baby boomers who had never used a pressure cooker began to discover the benefits of pressure-cooker cooking, and the number continues to grow today.

THE PRESSURE COOKER IN EUROPE

The use and development of pressure cookers in Europe, the world's largest market for this convenient cooking utensil, parallel to some extent those in the United States. During times of war, Europeans found the same benefits from pressure cooking as did their American counterparts. Suffering from major food shortages, a rapidly growing population after years of death and destruction, and lifestyle changes due to advances in technology, European housewives were concerned with providing their families with traditional home-cooked meals in a relatively short period of time. While Europeans, for the most part, have not embraced convenience foods as readily as their American counterparts, they too are concerned with saving time. In fact, the demand for pressure cookers in Europe was and has always been greater than in other parts of the world. It is quite commonplace to find not one but perhaps two or three pressure cookers of various sizes in European kitchens. Because of this demand and interest in pressure cooking, the major European manufacturers over the years have made the most improvements on the basic concept by developing new designs and incorporating new and improved safety features. In 1949, Kuhn-Rikon, of Switzerland, introduced the first spring-regulated valve, eliminating the need for a jiggler valve. This system is still used today and has been incorporated into the design and operation of most European-manufactured units. T-Fal, of France, began producing pressure cookers in 1953 and has been credited with introducing the first pressure cooker made from a stamped metal pot rather than a molded one. This strategic change eliminated the potential danger of structural weakness that used to lead to cracking and rupturing pots. Spain's Fagor, Magafesa, and Monix brand units dominate that national market. They tirelessly promote sophisticated units all over the world and have helped spur interest among American cooks with major distribution inroads in the United States.

THE BENEFITS OF COOKING IN A PRESSURE COOKER

Pressure cookers have many advantages over traditional cooking. First and foremost is speed. While it may take well over an hour or two to simmer a stew or to prepare a rich stock the conventional way, preparing those foods in a pressure cooker takes 50 to 70 percent less time. The speed at which a pressure cooker cooks means less energy is required and less heat is generated—especially important during hot weather. A nutritional advantage occurs because pressure cookers require less cooking liquid; water-soluble vitamins and minerals that are usually cooked away in traditional cooking methods are for the most part retained, and vegetables are also better able to keep their natural color and flavor.

HOW A PRESSURE COOKER WORKS

A pressure cooker is basically a metal pot with a lid. The lid components vital to the function and operation of the pressure cooker are the rubber sealing gasket, pressure regulator, and pressure-relief valves. When the lid is properly locked into place on the pressure cooker, an air- and steam-tight seal is created. As the cooking liquid in the pressure cooker is heated over high heat to the boiling point (212°F), steam is created. Since the steam cannot escape from the sealed pressure cooker, it remains trapped inside and pressure is created. The internal cooking temperature will vary depending on the different levels of pressure created by the trapped steam. The amount of pressure is measured in pounds of pressure per square inch (psi). Some pressure cookers only cook at high pressure, while others have two or three pressure levels. In developing and testing the recipes contained in this book, high pressure was used for each recipe with excellent results. For the most part, foods cooked under high pressure are cooked at 250°F, which is 38°F hotter than when food is boiled in a normal pot and speeds up the cooking process considerably.

PARTS OF A PRESSURE COOKER

There are three basic pressure cooker designs: the traditional "jiggler," or weight valve, pressure cooker (A), the developed weight valve pressure cooker (B), and the spring valve pressure cooker (C). While most of the components of these three different designs are similar, the main feature that distinguishes the three is the type of pressure regulator used. To determine the type you own, consult the printed materials provided by the manufacturer or locate the pressure regulator valve and identify the type of pressure regulator valve used by comparing it with the descriptions given on pages 21 to 23.

THE POT

Today's pressure-cooker pots are either made from stamped aluminum or stainless steel (usually high-quality 18/10 stainless, an alloy that contains 18 percent chromium

A. Jiggler- or Weight-Valve Pressure Cooker

Safety valve or vent and lid locking mechanism

Jiggler- or weight-valve pressure regulator

Vent pipe

Safety valve or vent

Lid handle

Rubber sealing gasket or ring

Pot handle

Stainless-steel or aluminum lid

Trivet

Three-ply bottom plate (in stainless-steel models only)

Stainless-steel or aluminum body

B. Developed Weight-Valve Pressure Cooker

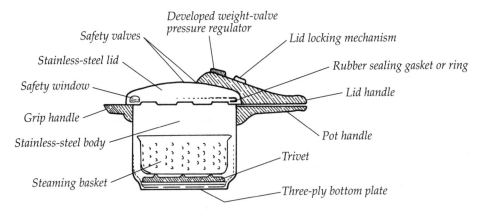

Safety valves

Developed weight-valve pressure regulator

Lid locking mechanism

Stainless-steel lid

Rubber sealing gasket or ring

Safety window

Lid handle

Grip handle

Pot handle

Stainless-steel body

Trivet

Steaming basket

Three-ply bottom plate

C. Spring-Valve Pressure Cooker

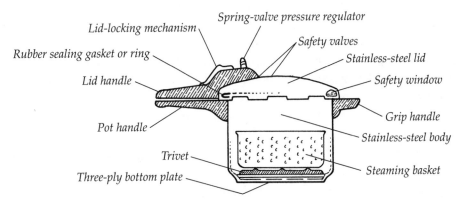

Lid-locking mechanism

Spring-valve pressure regulator

Safety valves

Rubber sealing gasket or ring

Stainless-steel lid

Lid handle

Safety window

Pot handle

Grip handle

Stainless-steel body

Trivet

Steaming basket

Three-ply bottom plate

and 10 percent nickel, making for a highly durable pot that is resistant to stains and corrosion). Units are available in a variety of sizes ranging from two to eight quarts; the most commonly used size, six quarts, can make four to eight servings, depending on the recipe. Even though stainless steel is an excellent retainer of heat, it does not distribute heat evenly. All stainless-steel pressure cookers, therefore, have a three-ply bottom plate where the unit comes in direct contact with the burner. Comprising a sheet of aluminum or copper sandwiched between two sheets of stainless steel, this plate distributes heat evenly, eliminating any hot or cold spots on the cooking surface of the pot.

All pressure cookers have two handles attached to the pot. Depending on the design of the pressure cooker, it may either have one long handle and perhaps a smaller griplike handle on the opposite end or two short griplike handles. The handles are used to steady the pressure cooker when locking or unlocking the lid and for moving the pressure cooker to or from the burner.

THE LID

The pressure-cooker lid is usually made from the same material as the pot, aluminum or stainless steel. The lids have one or two handles. Some have a handle that is long, to match a long one on the pot, others are griplike, and yet others have a knob. Some pressure-cooker lid handles also have a locking mechanism incorporated in the handle that must be activated in order to lock the lid in place. Others self-lock when the lid is turned into position. As a safety feature, most pressure cookers today, unlike the ones sold back in the forties, cannot be opened until the pressure has dropped to zero psi.

THE RUBBER SEALING GASKET OR RING

One of the features that Alfred Vischer invented in the 1940s and incorporated in his Flex-Seal Speed Cooker was a rubber sealing gasket, used to achieve a steam-proof seal when the lid was locked in place. This feature is now found on all pressure cookers and plays an important part in its operation. Since metal expands when heated, the rubber gasket provides a constant tight seal. In order to make sure the gasket performs as required, regularly check to make sure that it is clean and flexible. Over the course of time it can dry out and harden, losing its elasticity; it should then be replaced immediately. Most manufacturers suggest that the gasket be replaced at least once a year. You should never use your pressure cooker with a damaged gasket or without the rubber gasket properly positioned; the lid will not lock into place properly and/or steam will not build up and may even escape.

SAFETY VALVES

Today's pressure cookers have at least three safety valves that permit excess pressure to escape. Too much pressure builds up when high heat creates too much steam, a pressure regulator valve malfunctions or is obstructed, or the pressure cooker is overfilled, all of which are situations that should not occur under normal circumstances. While every model and brand is different, the basic concept behind the pressure-relief system is the same—safety.

All pressure cookers have a *pressure-regulator valve*. The purpose of the regulator is twofold. First and foremost, it indicates to the user that pressure is building up. Secondly, it is used to regulate the amount of pressure in the pot according to the recipe or instructions being used.

There are three types of pressure regulators: the traditional, "jiggler" or weight valve, the developed weight valve, and the spring valve. The pressure-regulator valve most commonly associated with pressure cookers is what has been referred to over the years as a *jiggler valve* (illustration A). This valve is usually a removable, heavy, round piece of metal that sits on the vent pipe located in the center of the lid. As pressure builds in the pressure cooker, steam comes out through the vent pipe causing the valve to jiggle or rock back and forth. The motion of the valve should be gentle and steady, with very little, if any, visible steam. You may also notice a low hissing sound. If the valve is rocking very quickly and if there is a considerable amount of steam and noise coming from the pressure-regulator valve and vent pipe, the burner heat is too high and excess pressure is venting. The heat should be lowered immediately before the safety valves are activated.

Other models have special weight valves that are either permanently positioned on the vent pipe or are positioned there and locked in place by the user. These are called *developed weight valves* (illustration B). When pressure is achieved, the developed weight valve raises up slightly and steam is emitted indicating to the user that maximum pressure has been reached and that the moment has arrived to adjust the burner heat to a level low enough to maintain pressure. This is indicated by just a faint stream of steam coming from the valve along with a very low hissing sound.

The other type of regulator valve used is the *spring valve* (illustration C). As pressure builds in the pressure cooker, a spring-loaded valve located in the lid compresses, usually raising some type of a pressure indicator into an upright position, allowing the user to see the level of pressure under which the food is cooking. Pressure levels may be indicated with colored markings or simple lines, and some units permit you to manually select the level of pressure by turning a knob on this kind of pressure-regulator valve. Since there are numerous variations of this system, check the instructions in your pressure cooker owner's manual to determine the different levels of pressure available and how to identify them.

Once the closed and locked pressure cooker is heated and pressure builds, steam will begin to come out of the pressure-regulator valve and a hissing sound will be heard. For safety purposes, if the burner heat is not adjusted and lowered, steam will continue to be released. As excessive pressure continues to build, the other safety valves will also activate.

There is usually a safety valve or vent located in the lid in addition to the pressure-regulator valve. This valve may be as simple as a rubber stopper or plug, or as sophisticated as a metal lug-nut–type valve. Depending on the design of the pressure cooker there is usually another safety valve located in the lid handle. Finally, some pressure cookers also have a rectangular cutout or safety window in the lid rim, which allows for expansion of the rubber gasket under excess pressure. As long as valves are kept unobstructed and clear of any food buildup so that they are in good working order, these features provide the user with a pressure cooker that is safer to use than ever before. See pages 25 and 30 for tips on care for safety valves.

STEAMING BASKET OR COOKING RACK

In addition to the pot and lid, most pressure cookers come with a steaming basket and trivet, or a steaming rack. This accessory can be used when you want to steam foods without letting them come in contact with the cooking liquid or water. When using the steaming basket or cooking rack, make sure that they are above the cooking liquid when in place—otherwise you will be defeating their purpose. Note, however, that when steaming foods that require a prolonged cooking time, you must be careful to use sufficient liquid so as not to scorch and damage the pressure cooker once the liquid evaporates. Basic cooking times and cooking liquid amounts for most foods are given in each chapter. In the event you do not have a steaming basket or rack, you can use the small, collapsible stainless-steel steaming baskets available at most housewares stores.

COOKING WITH A PRESSURE COOKER

Another notorious misconception about pressure-cooker cooking is that everything comes out overcooked, lifeless, and very wet. The technologically advanced pressure-regulating systems on even today's most basic models mean that much less liquid can be used. Because valves don't lose as much steam, you can use as little liquid as possible—just enough to develop and maintain the appropriate amount of steam and pressure while maximizing the flavor of the food.

The following pointers are some of the things that I have discovered over eighteen years of cooking with pressure cookers. By following these tips and by carefully reviewing all the instructional materials provided by the manufacturer, you will be well on your way to great results.

BEFORE YOU BEGIN COOKING

Each time you use your pressure cooker you should examine all the parts to make sure that everything is in working order. The following is a quick checklist.

1. Make sure that the pressure cooker was washed well after the last use. There should be no food or residue on the pot and lid. Make sure that the inner part of the lid rim, the outer rim on the pot, and the rubber gasket are clean. By doing so, you reduce the risk of the lid sticking when you open the pressure cooker after cooking.

2. Remove the rubber sealing gasket or ring to make sure that the rubber is still flexible and is not dried out. Check for any tears or cracks. If the rubber gasket shows any signs of being dry or damaged, do not use the pressure cooker. Replace the old part immediately with a new gasket or ring, readily obtainable from the manufacturer (see page 195 for manufacturers' consumer assistance phone numbers).

3. Check the safety valves. If your pressure cooker uses a jiggler valve or developed weight valve and has a vent pipe, stick a pipe cleaner or toothpick through the opening to make sure that the vent pipe is unobstructed and clean. Also check the jiggler valve, and all other valves, and remove any caked-on food residue. If your pressure cooker has a spring-regulated valve, press or pull gently on the valve (depending on the design) to make sure that it moves without any resistance. Since each manufacturer's design varies, check the owner's manual for the exact requirements for keeping the safety valves in working order.

LOADING THE PRESSURE COOKER

Since the pressure cooker needs space for the steam and pressure to build, never fill it more than two-thirds full. In fact, most pressure cookers have a two-thirds mark stamped on the inside of the pot, eliminating any guesswork. You should never pack solid foods into the pressure cooker, as that would defeat the purpose of fast cooking.

When preparing meat and poultry for cooking under pressure, brown them directly in the pressure cooker. By doing so, you will be adding extra flavor to the dish as well as adding extra color by browning the meat or poultry first. Always brown with the cover off and usually over high or medium-high heat, in order to sear the surface. Marinated foods should be well drained. All meat and poultry should be patted before browning. Be careful that the burner heat is not too high or you will burn the oil and scorch the pot. *Do not deep-fry* in a pressure cooker, regardless of whether the lid is on.

Lightly coat the steaming basket or cooking rack with vegetable oil when steaming foods, like fish, that might stick to the surface. Since some foods tend to react with aluminum, which causes them to discolor, remove the cooked food from the steaming basket or rack immediately.

POSITIONING AND LOCKING THE LID IN PLACE

Once all the ingredients are in the pressure cooker, you can begin cooking. Start by positioning the lid on the pressure cooker. There are two basic designs and systems for positioning and locking the lids in place.

You lock some lids in place by positioning them on the pressure cooker and turning them clockwise. These units usually have an arrow or other mark on the lid, which enables you to line it up in the right position. Simply lay the lid on the pressure cooker with the indicator mark lined up with the long pot handle. Making sure that the lid is sitting flush to the pot, carefully turn clockwise. Because of the tight fit of the rubber-seal gasket, some lids may offer more resistance than others. Never force the lid shut, since that is an indication that it probably is not lined up properly. If you do manage to close a misaligned lid, it will be very difficult, if not impossible, to reopen it, which will require contacting the manufacturer.

Other lid design systems used by pressure-cooker manufacturers are the self-locking lid and the screw-top lid. If your pressure cooker has a self-locking lid, simply position the lid on the pressure cooker in accordance with the manufacturer's instructions and lock in place. If your pressure cooker has a screw-top lid, position the lid on the pressure cooker and turn just until the locking bar on the lid slides under the two side brackets. Turn the locking-screw mechanism clockwise as far down as it will turn without forcing it.

If your pressure cooker uses a jiggler-type valve or a developed weight valve, place it where specified by the manufacturer once you have locked the lid in place. If your pressure cooker has a pressure selector that enables you to choose or adjust for the level of pressure desired, position it to or let it reach the proper setting according to the recipe you are following. All the recipes contained in this cookbook were developed using high pressure, which is usually the easiest level of pressure to reach and maintain.

Building and Adjusting Pressure

In order for the pressure cooker to build pressure, the cooking liquid in the pot has to be brought to a boil with the lid positioned and locked in place. As the cooking liquid boils, steam is produced. The trapped hot steam will build up and compress, creating pressure. Therefore, once your cooker is loaded and the lid is locked securely in place, raise the burner heat to high. As pressure builds, the pressure-regulator valve will activate in accordance with the specifications and features of your pressure cooker.

There are three ways you will know that high or maximum pressure has been reached:

1. On pressure cookers with spring-mechanism valves, the pressure-regulator valve will rise to indicate maximum pressure. On units with vent pipes, the jiggler valve or developed weight valve will either begin to rock and move, or will raise up, depending on the design.

2. You will notice a hissing sound coming from the pressure-regulator valve.

3. Steam will begin to escape from the spring-regulator valve—or in the case of pressure cookers with a jiggler valve or developed weight valve, from the vent pipe.

Once these three signs are evident, you will know that high or maximum pressure has been reached. Now, lower the burner heat as low as it takes for the pressure-regulator valve to indicate the level of pressure desired, either with a spring-loaded valve or developed weight valve in the appropriate position or with the jiggler valve continuing to rock. Depending on the design of your pressure cooker, you may notice a continuous or occasional low hissing sound, which may be barely audible, as well as a slight sign of steam. Do not lower the burner heat too much, otherwise the internal temperature of the pressure cooker will drop, and the steam and pressure will decrease, not allowing the unit to maintain the desired level of cooking pressure.

The following table shows the temperature-to-pressure ratios achieved when cooking in a pressure cooker.

PRESSURE	INTERNAL COOKING TEMPERATURE	PRESSURE
High	250°F	15 psi
Medium	235°F	10 psi
Low	220°F	5 psi

TIMING

Timing is key to achieving good results with a pressure cooker, and a kitchen timer is a valuable gadget to have on hand. Once the desired level of cooking pressure is reached, begin the cooking-time countdown. The cooking times given with each recipe, as well as the approximate cooking times provided in each chapter, begin once the desired level of pressure is reached.

Since overcooked food cannot be corrected, it is almost always better to err on the undercooked side by cooking an unfamiliar food for a shorter period of time than you think may be necessary. This way, you can always go back and continue cooking it a couple of minutes longer until the desired doneness is reached. You will also note that in some of the recipes, ingredients are added at different pressure cooking stages. Since foods need different amounts of cooking time, I prefer to start with those ingredients that require more time, release the pressure in the pressure cooker, add the additional ingredients, and then continue cooking. Even with the additional steps, you will still find that you are saving a considerable amount of time and will be able to avoid overcooking any one ingredient.

USING A PRESSURE COOKER AT HIGH ALTITUDES

The recipes in this cookbook were developed and tested at sea level. Since water and cooking liquids come to a boil more slowly at high altitudes, the cooking times must be longer. A good rule of thumb is to increase the cooking time by 5 percent for every 1,000 feet above the first 2,000 feet (3,000 feet above sea level, add 5 percent to cooking time; 4,000 feet, add 10 percent; and so on).

Since the cooking times increase at altitudes higher than 2,000 feet, you will also have to add more cooking liquid to compensate. There are no fixed rules, so try increasing the cooking liquid by approximately half the percentage of the additional cooking time. For example, if the cooking time is increased by 10 percent, increase the cooking liquid by 5 percent.

RELEASING PRESSURE

When the food has finished cooking, remove the pressure cooker from the burner. Even though the pressure cooker is no longer on the heat source, the contents will continue cooking until the temperature and level of pressure drop. There are three ways of releasing cooking pressure in a pressure cooker until you are able to open it:

1. The Natural-Release Method. Foods like stocks, tomato sauces, and certain cuts of meat benefit from continuing to cook in the pressure cooker as the pressure and temperature drop naturally after the unit is removed from the burner. The natural-release method can take anywhere from 10 minutes to over 20 minutes, depending on the kind of food in the pressure cooker and how much of it there is. You will know that the pressure has dropped completely once the spring-loaded pressure-regulator valve lowers completely or steam no longer comes out of the vent pipe on jiggler-valve and developed weight valve units.

2. The Cold-Water-Release Method. For the most part, you will want to lower and release the cooking pressure as quickly as possible in order to stop the cooking process. The quickest way to do this is to take the pressure cooker from the stove and carry it carefully to the sink by holding both handles. Place it in the sink and run cold water over the lid. This will stabilize the temperature and force the pressure to dissipate almost within seconds. You will normally hear a decompressing sound—almost like a swooshing "pop" —once all the pressure has been released.

3. The Automatic-Release Method. Some pressure cookers have an automatic release method, which enables you to release the pressure without having to place the pressure cooker under cold water. Consult the instructions provided by the manufacturer to see if this is the case with your specific model. If so, you can use this method instead when preparing any recipes in this book that call for the cold-water-release method.

OPENING THE PRESSURE COOKER

You can only open the pressure cooker after all the built-up pressure has been released. As a safety feature, UL now requires that all units have a safety lock that prevents the pot from being opened until there is no more pressure.

Since the food in the pressure cooker is extremely hot, you should take care in opening and removing the lid. Hold the griplike handle on the pot with one hand and turn the lid counterclockwise by grasping and turning the lid hard. Even though there is no further pressure in the pressure cooker, there will be some steam rising out and the food will be hot. Therefore, to avoid being burned, never hold your face over the pressure cooker as you remove the lid.

In the event you are unable to open the lid, repeat the cold-water-release method, as there still may be some remaining pressure.

CARE AND MAINTENANCE

The pressure cooker pot should be cleaned and maintained like any other piece of quality cookware.

To avoid staining an aluminum pressure cooker, do not let cooked food sit in the pot for an extended period. Wash the inside and outside of the pot and lid with mild dish-washing soap and a nonabrasive sponge after each use. Rinse well. Never immerse the lid in water, since it may affect and damage the safety valves. Never wash the pot, lid, or rubber gasket in the dishwasher. When washing the lid always remove the rubber-gasket seal or ring. Wash the gasket or ring separately with warm water and mild dish-washing soap.

Towel-dry all of the parts of the pressure cooker after washing. Reposition the washed and dried rubber-gasket seal or ring into the lid under the rim. Some manufacturers suggest that the pressure-regulator valve be disassembled and cleaned after each use. Check your manufacturer's instructions to see if this is the case, or if the manufacturer provides any other cleaning and maintenance instructions.

When storing the pressure cooker, *never* lock the lid in place, since you can damage the rubber gasket seal or ring or, worse yet, not be able to reopen the pressure cooker —moisture that may develop can create an almost permanent seal. Always store the lid upside down on top of the pot.

HELP IS BUT A PHONE CALL AWAY

If you should have questions regarding the proper use or care of your pressure cooker, don't forget that the best source of information is the manufacturer. All manufacturers have fully staffed customer-service departments with trained representatives who are happy to answer your questions. A list of various pressure cooker manufacturers is given on page 195, along with their customer-service phone numbers.

CONVERTING TRADITIONAL RECIPES
FOR USE IN THE PRESSURE COOKER

It is easy to adapt your favorite recipe for use in a pressure cooker. For the most part, soups, stews, braised and slow-roasted meats and poultry, steamed and braised vegetables, dried beans and legumes, and slow-simmered recipes like tomato sauce and fruit preserves, provide the best results. When converting a recipe, always refer to the approximate cooking times at the beginning of each recipe chapter for the type of food being prepared. In addition to giving cooking times, this information also provides guidelines for the amount of cooking liquid required.

When cooking meats and poultry, brown them well in the pressure cooker using at least three tablespoons of vegetable or olive oil or other fat. Sauté onions, garlic, or other vegetables called for in the recipe. Add the remaining ingredients and at least three-fourths of a cup of cooking liquid, such as stock, diluted tomato puree, or wine, depending on the length of the cooking time. Bear in mind that the amount of cooking liquid will probably be much less than that needed in traditional cooking, since you will be cooking in a sealed pot for a much shorter period of time, making for less evaporation. You must, however, use sufficient liquid, since the pressure cooker is constantly building steam during the entire cooking process. If you run out of liquid and continue cooking, the food will burn.

Soups are quick and easy to prepare in the pressure cooker. Add beans, meat, poultry, or seafood to the pressure cooker along with any desired vegetables, herbs, and spices. Add the cooking liquid, usually water or stock, filling the pressure cooker no more than two-thirds full. Consult the approximate cooking times at the beginning of each chapter for basic cooking information.

Foods like tomato sauce and fruit preserves cook to perfection in a pressure cooker, saving 50 to 70 percent in cooking time. When preparing tomato sauce, sauté finely chopped onion and/or garlic in olive oil. Add and brown the meats as specified in the recipe. Add the strained or pureed tomatoes, filling the pressure cooker only two-thirds full. Position the lid and lock in place. Cook under high pressure, 20 to 30 minutes. Remove from heat and let the pressure drop naturally.

To make fruit preserves, prepare the fruit as indicated in your recipe. Place the fruit in the pressure cooker with the desired quantity of sugar. Let sit one hour to release the natural juices of fruit. Bring to a boil, uncovered. Stir well and add the other ingredients as indicated in your recipe. Position lid and lock in place. Cook under high pressure for up to 8 minutes. Remove from heat and let pressure drop naturally.

Bear in mind that there are no universal guidelines for converting recipes for pressure-cooker use. Trial and error will come into play until you understand how a pressure cooker cooks. Because it can always be cooked longer, if need be, it is always better to undercook rather than to overcook food.

THE PRESSURE COOKER AND THE MEDITERRANEAN DIET

My first encounter with the pressure cooker was in 1977. I was twenty years old and living in Spain as a language student at the University of Seville. During the two years I lived in Seville I shared an apartment with three Spanish students. Since I was the only one who knew my way around the kitchen, I was the appointed cook. We were all on tight budgets, and it was my job to shop and prepare three meals a day on less than $50 a week. That was no easy task, even in Spain in the late 1970s. Fortunately bread, which makes up a fundamental part of every meal in Spain, was very inexpensive and helped sustain us, especially toward the end of the month! But the thing that really saved us was a Fagor eight-liter, jiggler-valve pressure cooker we found in the apartment that we had rented. Having never seen nor used one before, I at first put it away in the back of the cupboard. After spending a few weekends with the family of one of my roommates, I became intrigued with the delicious meals his mother produced from this very noisy pot with the twirling valve. After getting over my initial curiosity, I began to spend as much time as possible taking copious notes on how to cook in a pressure cooker. After a few batches of overcooked beans and vegetables, I finally got the hang of it, and before I knew it I was preparing almost every conceivable Spanish dish possible and even a few creations of my own in my trusty pressure cooker.

When I returned to New York and set up house on my own, one of the first things I did was to buy an inexpensive aluminum pressure cooker. I felt like a bit of a pioneer; this was 1979 and no one I knew owned a pressure cooker or had ever used one. Nevertheless, I continued cooking under pressure as often as possible, amazing (and perhaps scaring) both family and friends.

Since I had learned to use a pressure cooker in Europe, where more pressure cookers are manufactured, sold, and used than anywhere else in the world (this is especially true in the Mediterranean basin), I was extremely disappointed with the lack of appealing pressure cooker recipes available in this country. For lack of other alternatives, I began to adapt and cook in the pressure cooker some of the foods I had grown up eating—to great success. I became even more enthusiastic when information on the Mediterranean Diet was first published in the mid-1990s. It seems that Mom was right: all of the meatless dishes of pasta with every conceivable type of bean and vegetable that she prepared while I was growing up were being promoted as part of a nutritionally superior diet. I set out to apply this information to the pressure cooker and began preparing as many different types of Mediterranean and

Mediterranean-inspired dishes as possible. The results of years of delicious pressure-cooked meals are gathered in this book.

Over the years the number of pressure cookers available at retail has expanded from just a handful to more than twenty different models. I have ventured beyond the Presto classic and now have an impressive collection of pressure cookers of varying sizes and designs. I have also learned to appreciate the pleasure of cooking in the new European, stainless-steel, spring-valve and developed weight valve regulated models. Nevertheless, I have never strayed from its origins and continue preparing essentially Mediterranean foods in this, my most valuable of kitchen tools, the pressure cooker.

THE MEDITERRANEAN DIET

A simple cuisine with peasant origins, Mediterranean food is never pretentious. We now know and understand the nutritional benefits of this diet that is based on fresh fruits and vegetables, dried beans and legumes, grains and cereals, seafood, olive oil, and only the minimum animal protein and fat.

In the early 1990s, leading international scientists and nutritionists created daily dietary recommendations based on life-expectancy research conducted in the Mediterranean region since the early 1960s. According to Dr. Dimitrios Trichopoulos, chairman of the department of epidemiology at the Harvard School of Public Health, "People of the Mediterranean countries, the Greeks, Italians, Spaniards, have lower incidence of coronary disease and several forms of cancer. Their life expectancy is actually longer than it is in the United States and several other central and northern European nations." The experts contend that the traditional Mediterranean diet, along with a low to moderate intake of wine, contribute directly to the lower levels of heart disease and cancer. Based on this research, the Mediterranean Diet Pyramid (page 34) was developed and introduced by the World Health Organization, the Harvard School of Public Health, and Oldways Preservation & Exchange Trust, a Boston-based, nonprofit educational organization dedicated to promoting healthy, environmentally sustainable food and preserving the agricultural traditions of many cultures. According to Dr. Frank Sacks, associate professor of medicine at the Harvard Medical School, "More than half the area of the pyramid is made up of plant-based foods. It reflects the fact that in traditional Mediterranean areas, beef and other meats are not at the center of the plate. They are peripheral and consumed occasionally. That seems to be a reasonable way to eat and keep coronary disease rates down."

The Mediterranean Diet advocates the liberal use of olive oil as the primary source of fat in a healthy diet. Olive oil has been the fat of choice in the Mediterranean region for centuries, and researchers have discovered a direct correlation between it

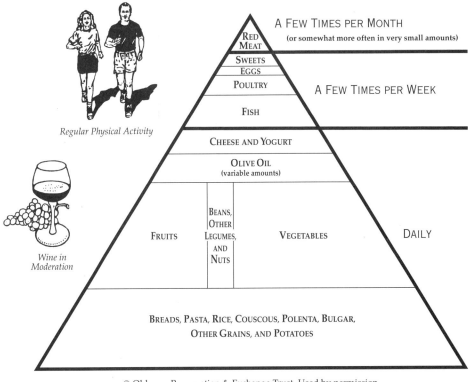

© Oldways Preservation & Exchange Trust. Used by permission.

MEDITERRANEAN DIET PYRAMID

and the low incidence of heart disease in Mediterranean peoples. A monosaturated oil, it tends to lower artery-clogging LDL cholesterol while maintaining beneficial levels of protective HDL cholesterol. Olive oil is also rich in vitamin E, an antioxidant believed to neutralize the free radicals that flow in the blood stream damaging cells and causing tumors to form. Since olive oil is a fat and thus high in calories, its benefits can be counterproductive if moderate exercise does not play a part in a healthy lifestyle and daily routine.

Other primary components of the region's cuisines, such as dried beans and legumes, provide valuable high levels of protein, complex carbohydrates, and fiber, and replace meat as the primary source of protein. Leafy green vegetables and yellow vegetables high in betacarotene, like carrots and squash, may also reduce the incidence of certain types of cancer.

Researchers also believe that the lack of stress in the Mediterranean rural lifestyle contributes significantly to the low incidence of heart disease, since it has been documented that stress raises cholesterol levels. Since the inhabitants of the Mediterranean consider meals to be a fundamentally communal experience, they are usually leisurely, eaten with family and friends where the surroundings and company are as important as the food. Therefore, taken collectively, the Mediterranean Diet is much more than the preparation and consumption of food—it is a way of eating *and* a way of life.

Traditional Mediterranean Regional Ingredients

The Mediterranean region is made up of fifteen countries in three continents, all bordering on or influenced by the Mediterranean Sea. The area has been blessed with fertile fields and hillsides that provide the optimum geography and climate for growing the wonderful fruits, vegetables, and herbs that have made the diverse cuisines of this area world-renowned and much appreciated. The rich culinary heritage is also derived from the sea that gives its name to that region. The following are some of the outstanding ingredients that make up the Mediterranean diet and cuisine.

Artichokes

This quintessential Mediterranean vegetable appears throughout the different cuisines of the region. Actually the flower bud of the artichoke plant, large artichokes grow directly from the main stem of the plant; smaller or baby artichokes grow from the side shoots.

When purchasing artichokes, make sure that they are firm when squeezed and make a squeaky sound, an indication that the leaves are plump and crisp. Check the stem and base to see that there are no signs of worm holes, as worms can burrow in the center or heart and cause considerable damage. The outer leaves should be an even shade of green ranging from a soft hue in the spring to olive color in the fall. The artichokes should also be free of any black or dark-brown blemishes. Since the outer leaves are tough they should be torn off and discarded before cooking. Cut artichokes will discolor if not cooked immediately. Soak them in a water and lemon juice mixture to maintain their bright color until you are ready to cook them.

Capers

Capers are the flower bud of a bush native to the Mediterranean. The small buds are picked, sun dried, and then either pickled in vinegar brine or packed in salt. Although now cultivated, caper bushes still grow wild in many remote areas in the Mediterranean region.

Preserved capers have a pungent, distinctive flavor and are added to prepared dishes in small amounts. Capers come in many different sizes. I prefer to use the smallest I can find. Since they can be salty, always rinse them under cold water in a fine mesh strainer before using. Capers are available in most supermarkets.

Cereals and grains

A fundamental part of the Mediterranean diet, cereals and grains are high in complex carbohydrates and an integral part of a healthy diet regardless of where one lives. These foods are much appreciated in most of the region in several different forms.

It should come as no surprise that Italians are the largest consumers of pasta, with an estimated annual consumption of approximately 55 pounds per person. Recorded history shows that pasta has been eaten in the Italian peninsula since the days of the ancient Romans, who enjoyed dumplings and sheets of lasagnalike pasta, which were boiled, fried, or baked. It was not until the Saracen Arabic domination of Sicily in A.D. 831, however, that dried forms of pasta were first produced commercially.

Cornmeal in the form of a savory mush or porridge is enjoyed in Italy where it is known as *polenta.* The same food in Spain is known as *gachas* and in Portugal, *papas de milho.*

Grain also appears at least three times a day in the daily bread of the region. In fact, it would be unheard of to serve a meal without bread, or, as the Spaniards say, *"Es más largo que un día sin pan."* (It is as long as a day without bread.) The favored breads of the region vary from country to country and area to area; however, for the most part they are all raised loaves made from locally grown wheat with a hard crust and chewy crumb.

Another key grain, rice—especially the short grain variety of the region—was introduced to the Mediterranean by the Moors soon after their invasion of southern Europe in the eighth century. The best-known of the short-grained rices are the Italian arborio and the variety of rice grown in Valencia, Spain. Used to make Italian risotto, Spanish paella, and Arabic pilaf, rice is also added to other ingredients as a stuffing for vegetables, or prepared with milk, sugar, and spices for dessert.

Couscous, a staple of North African cuisine, is a pasta made from semolina. The coarse flour is mixed with water to form a crumbly mixture that is passed through a flat-bottomed sieve to form small particles of pasta that are then air-dried.

While Arabic cooks prepare couscous by steaming it in a cone-shaped cooking vessel called a *couscoussière,* couscous is available at most supermarkets in an instant version that only needs to be mixed in a saucepan with boiling cooking liquid and then allowed to rest a few minutes to soften. Due to its excellent capacity to absorb liquids and sauces, couscous is the perfect foil for Maghreb stews like *tagine*, which is made with lamb, beef, chicken, or vegetables.

Dried legumes and beans

For centuries these have been the main source of protein in this region. Beans, lentils, and dried peas are used in soups and stews and are also used to make spreads and dips.

If possible, purchase dried legumes and beans from a retailer whose stock turns over rapidly since older legumes and beans take longer to cook. Always wash them in a colander with cold water and pick over them to remove any foreign particles like small pebbles. Since beans cook quickly in a pressure cooker, there is no need to presoak them overnight. It is essential, however, that they soak at least one hour in boiling water before cooking, which will help the beans to begin hydrating. It is not necessary to soak lentils and split peas. Adding an onion, cloves, and a bay leaf to the cooking water adds extra flavor to the cooking beans. Never add salt to beans and dried legumes at the beginning of the cooking process, it will harden them. Salt can either be added toward the end of the cooking process or along with the other ingredients with which the beans are being prepared.

Dairy

As we know them, dairy products are not as prevalent in the Mediterranean diet, because of the absence of large expanses of grazing land for cows. However, many milk-based products are made from goat's or sheep's milk which is more readily available, since these animals do not require large pastures and survive quite well on the dry grass and brush of the Mediterranean region.

Cow's milk is generally consumed in small quantities, usually only at breakfast. Butter is also used only in small amounts, and in some regions is almost nonexistent. Cheese, however, is very prevalent, especially in southern Europe, where hard cheeses like Parmesan and Pecorino Romano are either grated over prepared dishes or used in cooking. Cheeses made from goat's, sheep's, or cow's milk, or a combination of milks, and cured to various stages have been a fundamental part of the Mediterranean diet for centuries. Yogurt is also consumed in varying amounts according to the country. Ice cream, while greatly enjoyed, is only consumed on occasion, and only in small quantities.

Eggplant

This native of India was probably introduced to the Mediterranean region by Arabic traders. An extremely adaptable vegetable, eggplant is combined with other vegetables from the region to be pickled, sautéed, fried, roasted, and baked. When buying eggplant look for a well-rounded, symmetrical eggplant with satin-smooth skin free of brown blemishes or soft spots.

Eggplant comes in a variety of sizes and shapes ranging from round to oval, long and skinny to short and fat. Colors range from purple-black to light purple to white with purple stripes to plain white. Generally, smaller eggplants are sweeter. Some recipes suggest sprinkling the cut-up or sliced eggplant with salt to draw out some of its moisture. This serves two purposes. Eggplant is very absorbent; when its juices are released the eggplant loses much of its capacity to absorb oil when fried or sautéed. Salting also seems to eliminate some of the eggplant's natural bitterness. Eggplant does not have to be peeled when prepared, unless called for in the recipe.

Eggs

This vital source of protein in the Mediterranean is consumed not as a breakfast food but as the main part of lunch or dinner. Eggs are made into omelets like the famous *tortilla española* from Spain or the Italian frittata, or simply fried in olive oil to accompany simple vegetable dishes. They are also beaten and added to fortify soups and used in numerous recipes. Eggs are combined with olive oil to make mayonnaise, which is then used to prepare potato salads or mixed with garlic for Provençal *aïoli* or Spanish *alioli,* which is served with fish dishes or boiled potatoes.

Fish and shellfish

Seafood is enjoyed throughout the Mediterranean region. Sadly, due to overfishing and the polluted conditions of the Mediterranean Sea, most of the fish and shellfish sold in the region today comes from the Atlantic and Pacific Oceans. Hake, cod, tuna, mullet, mackerel, sardines, squid, octopus, clams, mussels, and shrimp are some of the more popular kinds of seafood in Mediterranean kitchens. As with most Mediterranean cooking, their preparation is kept simple in order to retain their natural flavor. Accompaniments may include only a simple sprinkling of extra-virgin olive oil and lemon juice or a quickly cooked, garlicky tomato sauce.

Garlic and onions

We remember the fish we did eat in Egypt freely; the cucumbers, and the melons and leeks, and onions, and the garlic. (Nm. 11:5.) During their forty years of wandering the followers of Moses lamented the loss of these favorite foods while in the desert, and I am certain that today's Mediterranean cooks would share the same sentiment if deprived of the beloved garlic and onions that make up the backbone of many recipes. When unpeeled cloves of garlic are added to recipes they impart a gentle, less forceful flavor than when chopped, minced, or crushed. Onion adds a mellow sweetness, especially when sautéed slowly. No cuisine of the region would be complete without these two foods.

Herbs and spices

Flavorings used in Mediterranean cooking are either indigenous to the area or were introduced by the Moors during their domination of the region during the Middle Ages. Herbs such as thyme, oregano, mint, and sage still grow wild and play an important part in the seasoning of regional dishes, as do parsley and cilantro. Exotic spices like saffron and cumin are used judiciously by frugal cooks. Basil plays an important role in the cuisine of Italy and Provence, where it is used to flavor tomato-based sauces and in preparing Italy's pesto—or as it is known in Provence, pistou.

Meat and poultry

While present in the diet of the Mediterranean region, these foods are usually eaten in much smaller quantities and less frequently than in other developed parts of the world. Chicken, pork, and goat are the meats of choice in the Iberian Peninsula; Italians prize chicken, veal, and lamb; the Greeks prefer chicken and lamb; and those in the Moslem countries of the Mediterranean choose chicken, lamb, and goat. Wild game is also prevalent, especially rabbit, wild boar, and forest birds. For the most part, meat and poultry are not the main focus of the meal—rather, they are used to flavor or accompany the other components of the dish.

Cured meats are greatly appreciated throughout the region. Cured ham like Portuguese *presunto,* Spanish *jamón serrano,* and Italian prosciutto are either eaten sliced with bread or with fruits like figs or melon, which provide a counterpoint to the saltiness of the ham, or they are added to dishes in small quantities for flavor. Sausages, both fresh and dried, are also an important component of the region's diet.

Olive oil

Olive oil is the main source of fat in traditional Mediterranean cooking. It is believed that the ancient Arabs were the first to cultivate olive trees (around 6000 B.C.), after which the planting of olive trees began to spread throughout the region. With fruit that can be preserved in brine or cured in salt, oil that can be extracted from the olive, and its prized wood, the olive tree has long been held in high esteem.

Olive oil is believed to play a key role in maintaining a healthy diet in the Mediterranean region. A monosaturate, olive oil is cholesterol-free and is thought to help eliminate cholesterol from the blood by carrying it to the liver. Olive trees cover most of the region, and both the variety of tree and the conditions under which they grow influence the quality and flavor of the oil. There are three basic retail grades of olive oil available. The most expensive is generally extra-virgin olive oil, which is obtained from the fruit of the olive tree only by mechanical or physical means. In order to be classified as extra-virgin, the oil can only be from the first cold pressing of the olives and have an acidity level no greater than one percent. Virgin olive oil is also from the first cold pressing; by law, however, it can have an acidity level of between 1.0 percent and 3.3 percent. Olive oil, generally the least expensive, is a blend of heat-refined and chemically refined olive oil and virgin olive oil having an acidity level of less than 1.5 percent.

For general cooking like sautéeing and frying, use virgin olive oil or olive oil. Use the richer, usually more flavorful, extra-virgin olive oil for dressing cooked foods or when indicated in a given recipe.

Brine or salt-cured olives are also popular in this region, whether eaten simply out of hand or added as an ingredient to a recipe. The variety of olives and favored methods of preparation vary from area to area.

Peppers

This New World vegetable was brought back to the Mediterranean region by Spanish explorers during the sixteenth century. Generally used as a flavoring agent, peppers are also roasted, fried, and baked. Sweet and hot peppers are also dried and added to dishes for taste. Nevertheless, Mediterranean cooking, with a few exceptions, is not known for its spiciness. Paprika, a spice made from ground, dried red peppers, is also used extensively in its milder version in the cooking of the Iberian Peninsula.

There are two types of peppers predominately used in Mediterranean cooking. The light green, long and thin pepper, sometimes called Italian peppers or cubanelle, are thin-skinned and very flavorful and are usually fried or sautéed. Bell peppers are usually stuffed when green and either sautéed or roasted when totally mature and bright red in color.

Potatoes

Introduced to the Mediterranean region from the Americas, whence they originated, potatoes were brought to Europe as a cheap source of nutrition for the poor. Today, they are enjoyed throughout the region in various guises. Thin-cut shoestring potatoes, fried in olive oil, are universally popular and are served as an accompaniment to meat and poultry entrées or are served, as in Spain, with fried eggs. Boiled potatoes are also eaten plain in Portugal as a side dish. They are also cooked with other vegetables, turned into salads, and added to soups and stews.

Tomatoes

Originally thought to be poisonous when brought to Europe by Spanish explorers in the sixteenth century, tomatoes would not be accepted as a food until the nineteenth century. The tomato has obviously made up for lost time and has become one of the most important ingredients used today in Mediterranean cooking. While they are available year round, fresh tomatoes when in season and vine-ripened impart the best flavor. When using canned tomatoes, choose a quality brand for best results.

Vegetables

Vegetables, in general, make up a fundamental part of the diet of the Mediterranean inhabitants. In addition to those mentioned above, the following are also prevalent and appreciated: green beans; carrots; all types of leafy greens, such as spinach, escarole, broccoli di rape, cilantro, and parsley; and wild greens like dandelion. Pumpkin and squash as well as cauliflower, broccoli, and cabbage are used in varying amounts, depending on the region.

PART TWO

MEDITERRANEAN RECIPES IN THE PRESSURE COOKER

STOCKS AND SOUPS

Stock is a wonderful base for preparing flavorful and rich soups and sauces. Stock is traditionally simmered for hours in order to extract maximum flavor from the different ingredients, but stock prepared in a pressure cooker takes up to 70 percent less cooking time. Since stock freezes well, it makes sense to have a few batches on hand to take out whenever the urge strikes for a bowl of homemade soup or when stock is called for in a recipe.

The four recipes that immediately follow are for the most commonly used stocks, made from vegetables, chicken, beef, or fish.

RICH VEGETABLE STOCK

1 large onion, thinly sliced
1 large leek, trimmed and washed, green and white parts chopped
4 unpeeled cloves garlic, crushed
2 large carrots, coarsely chopped
2 stalks celery, coarsely chopped
1 medium turnip, peeled and coarsely chopped
1 large potato, peeled and coarsely chopped

1 large vine-ripened tomato, peeled, seeded, and coarsely chopped, or 2 canned plum tomatoes, seeded and chopped
6 sprigs parsley
1 bay leaf
1/2 teaspoon whole black peppercorns
9 cups water

Place all the ingredients in the pressure cooker. Position the lid and lock in place. Place over high heat and bring to high pressure. Adjust heat to stabilize pressure, and cook 15 minutes. Remove from heat and let pressure drop naturally. Once pressure has been released, open the pressure cooker. Strain the stock through a fine-mesh strainer, pressing as much liquid from the vegetables as possible before discarding them. Season with salt, if desired.

APPROXIMATELY 8 CUPS

APPROXIMATE NUTRITIONAL ANALYSIS PER 8-OUNCE CUP
39 calories, 1g protein, 9g carbohydrates, 0g fat, 0mg cholesterol, 36mg sodium

RICH CHICKEN STOCK

2¹/₂ to 3 pounds chicken bones
   with meat, including backs,
   wings, and necks, all visible fat
   and skin removed
1 large onion, thinly sliced
2 large leeks, trimmed, washed
   well, and chopped
2 large carrots, coarsely chopped
2 stalks celery, coarsely chopped
2 sprigs celery leaves

1 large vine-ripened tomato,
   peeled, seeded, and coarsely
   chopped, or 2 canned plum
   tomatoes, seeded and chopped
4 ¹/₄-inch-thick slices of peeled
   gingerroot
4 sprigs parsley
¹/₂ teaspoon whole black
   peppercorns
9 cups water

Rinse the chicken under running water. Place the chicken and the remaining ingredients in the pressure cooker. Position the lid and lock in place. Place over high heat and bring to high pressure. Adjust heat to stabilize pressure and cook 30 minutes. Remove from heat and let pressure drop naturally. Once the pressure has dropped, open the pressure cooker. Remove the chicken pieces with a slotted spoon and discard. Strain the stock through a fine-mesh strainer, pressing as much liquid from the vegetables as possible before discarding them. Season with salt, if desired.

APPROXIMATELY 8 CUPS

APPROXIMATE NUTRITIONAL ANALYSIS PER 8-OUNCE CUP

206 calories, 21g protein, 5g carbohydrates, 1g fat, 65mg cholesterol, 88mg sodium

RICH BEEF STOCK

3 pounds beef bones
3 tablespoons vegetable oil
1 large onion, thinly sliced
4 carrots, coarsely chopped
3 ribs celery, coarsely chopped
3 sprigs celery leaves
2 vine-ripened tomatoes, peeled,
   seeded, and coarsely chopped,
   or 3 canned plum tomatoes,
   seeded and chopped

$\frac{1}{2}$ teaspoon whole black
   peppercorns
9 cups water

Preheat the oven to 400°F. Rinse the beef bones under running water and pat dry. Place the bones in a single layer in a large roasting pan. Drizzle with the oil and toss to coat. Roast approximately 1 to 1½ hours, or until deep golden brown. Remove from the pan with a slotted spoon, allowing all the grease and oil to drip off.

Place the roasted bones, along with the remaining ingredients, in the pressure cooker. Position the lid and lock in place. Place over high heat and bring to high pressure. Adjust heat to stabilize pressure and cook 25 minutes. Remove from heat and let pressure drop naturally. Once the pressure has dropped, open the pressure cooker. Remove the bones with a slotted spoon and discard. Strain the stock through a fine-mesh strainer, pressing as much liquid from the vegetables as possible before discarding them. Season with salt, if desired.

APPROXIMATELY 8 CUPS

APPROXIMATE NUTRITIONAL ANALYSIS PER 8 OUNCE CUP
307 calories, 13g protein, 3g carbohydrates, 27g fat, 54mg cholesterol, 44mg sodium

RICH FISH STOCK

2 pounds fish skeletons with
  heads (use white fish for best
  results)
1 large onion, thinly sliced
2 carrots, coarsely chopped
2 stalks celery, coarsely chopped

2 cloves
½ bay leaf
½ teaspoon whole black
  peppercorns
9 cups water

Rinse the fish bones and heads under running water. Place the fish and the remaining ingredients in the pressure cooker. Position the lid and lock in place. Place over high heat and bring to high pressure. Adjust heat to stabilize pressure and cook 15 minutes. Remove from heat and let pressure drop naturally. Once the pressure has dropped, open the pressure cooker. Remove the bones and heads with a slotted spoon and discard. Strain the stock through a fine-mesh strainer, pressing as much liquid from the vegetables as possible before discarding. Season with salt, if desired.

APPROXIMATELY 8 CUPS

APPROXIMATE NUTRITIONAL ANALYSIS PER 8-OUNCE CUP

210 calories, 28g protein, 3g carbohydrates, 9g fat, 87mg cholesterol, 99mg sodium

CHICKEN SOUP WITH LEMON AND MINT
Canja

PORTUGAL

Lemon juice is a favorite addition to chicken soup in the Mediterranean region. Canja, a soup enjoyed throughout Portugal, is a fine example of this. The mint in this recipe adds a refreshing taste to this favorite.

1 split chicken breast with bone, about ¾ to 1 pound
1 large onion, peeled
1 2-inch strip of lemon zest
1 sprig fresh mint
8 cups water
3 teaspoons salt

⅓ cup long-grain rice
1 tablespoon fresh-squeezed lemon juice
Pinch of freshly ground black pepper
8 fresh mint leaves

Place the chicken breast, onion, lemon zest, mint sprig, water, and salt in the pressure cooker. Position the lid and lock in place. Place over high heat and bring to high pressure. Adjust heat to stabilize pressure and cook 20 minutes. Remove from heat and lower pressure using the cold-water-release method. Open the pressure cooker. Remove the chicken breast with a slotted spoon. Remove and discard the skin from the chicken. Bone the chicken and shred the meat. Cover and set aside.

Strain the stock through a fine-mesh strainer. Discard the onion, lemon zest and mint sprig. Pour the stock back into the pressure cooker. Add the rice and lemon juice. Reposition the lid and lock in place. Place over high heat and bring to high pressure. Adjust the heat to stabilize pressure and cook 5 minutes. Lower pressure using the cold-water-release method. Open the pressure cooker. Test rice to see if it is cooked. If rice is still hard, let soup simmer, uncovered, until rice is done. Taste and adjust for salt. Add the shredded chicken and black pepper. To serve, float 2 mint leaves on top of each bowl.

4 SERVINGS

APPROXIMATE NUTRITIONAL ANALYSIS PER SERVING
151 calories, 11g protein, 21g carbohydrates, 3g fat, 21mg cholesterol, 1656mg sodium

CHICKEN SOUP WITH EGG AND LEMON JUICE
Avgolemono Soupa

It is very common in Mediterranean countries to add beaten eggs and lemon juice to chicken soup before serving it. In the following classic Aegean version, which goes back to the days of the ancient Greeks, the eggs are beaten separately until the whites are stiff. The egg-and-lemon mixture is then stirred into the hot soup, adding both body and rich flavor.

6 cups Rich Chicken Stock (page 47), or canned chicken broth
1/3 cup short-grain rice

3 large eggs, separated
Juice of 1 large lemon

Pour the stock into the pressure cooker and add the rice. Position the lid and lock in place. Place over high heat and bring to high pressure. Adjust heat to stabilize pressure and cook 10 minutes. Remove from heat and lower pressure using the cold-water-release method. Open the pressure cooker. Place on the burner and maintain at a simmer

In a large mixing bowl, beat the egg whites until stiff. Add the egg yolks and beat until light. Gradually stir in the lemon juice. Slowly pour 2 cups of the simmering stock into the egg mixture, stirring constantly. Pour the beaten-egg mixture into the stock, stirring constantly. Remove the pressure cooker from the heat and continue stirring 1 minute. Serve immediately.

6 SERVINGS

APPROXIMATE NUTRITIONAL ANALYSIS PER SERVING

131 calories, 15g protein, 7g carbohydrates, 5g fat, 110mg cholesterol, 1624mg sodium

ROMAN EGG-DROP SOUP
Stracciatella

Stracciatella derives its name from *straccetti,* which means "little rags" in Italian. When the beaten eggs and cheese are whisked into the hot chicken soup, they break into small, torn pieces. This simple-to-prepare soup is as delicious as it is elegant.

8 cups Rich Chicken Stock (page 47)
4 large eggs
1/2 cup freshly grated Parmesan cheese

2 tablespoons finely minced parsley

Bring the chicken stock to a boil. In a medium-sized mixing bowl beat the eggs. Add the grated Parmesan cheese and parsley to the eggs. Slowly pour the egg mixture into the stock, whisking vigorously 1 to 2 minutes, or until the egg is broken into fine pieces. Serve immediately.

8 SERVINGS

APPROXIMATE NUTRITIONAL ANALYSIS PER SERVING
141 calories, 17g protein, 3g carbohydrates, 7g fat, 115mg cholesterol, 1701mg sodium

GARLIC SOUP
Sopa de Ajo

This simple soup of humble origin is so prevalent in Spanish cooking that even the great Spanish master Velázquez made it the focus of one of his most famous paintings, *Vieja cocinando* (Old Lady Cooking, 1618), which portrays an old woman stirring eggs into a shallow terra-cotta cooking vessel, or *cazuela*, of broth.

Comprising those elements most appreciated and accessible to Spanish cooks—garlic, eggs, bread, paprika, saffron, and olive oil—*sopa de ajo* is comfort food for Spaniards.

3 tablespoons extra-virgin olive oil
6 large cloves garlic, peeled
4 ¼-inch-thick slices day-old
  French bread
2 cups Rich Chicken Stock (page 47), or canned chicken broth

4 cups water
1 tablespoon paprika
¼ teaspoon ground cumin
5 strands of saffron (optional)
2 large eggs, lightly beaten

Heat the olive oil in the pressure cooker over medium heat. Add the garlic and sauté on all sides until golden. Remove from the pressure cooker and set aside. Add the bread and brown on both sides until golden. Remove and set aside.

Pour the stock and water in the pressure cooker. Stir in the browned garlic, paprika, and cumin and the saffron, if desired. Position the lid and lock in place. Place over high heat and bring to high pressure. Adjust heat to stabilize pressure and cook 5 minutes. Remove from heat and lower pressure using the cold-water-release method. Open the pressure cooker. Remove the garlic with a slotted spoon. Mash with a fork in a small bowl with a spoonful or two of the broth. Stir the mashed garlic into the soup. Taste and adjust for salt.

Bring the soup to a simmer. Slowly pour the beaten eggs into the hot soup, stirring constantly in one direction, allowing the eggs to form medium-sized strands.

Place a slice of fried bread in each soup bowl. Ladle the hot soup over the fried bread.

4 SERVINGS

APPROXIMATE NUTRITIONAL ANALYSIS PER SERVING

292 calories, 15g protein, 23g carbohydrates, 16g fat, 108mg cholesterol, 1448mg sodium

KALE SOUP
Caldo Gallego

♦ *Caldo Verde, Portugal*

This thick, hearty, country soup is chock full of vitamin-rich kale, a leafy green much appreciated throughout Portugal and the northwestern Spanish region of Galicia. Although these two parts of the Mediterranean region share many common bonds, their preferences in preparing this soup vary. I have provided both versions here.

4 tablespoons olive oil
1 large onion, finely chopped
1 clove garlic, peeled and minced
3 medium boiling potatoes, peeled
  and thinly sliced

8 cups water
2 teaspoons salt
1 pound kale, trimmed of all thick
  stems and coarsely shredded

For *caldo gallego*

4-ounce slice Spanish serrano ham
  or Italian prosciutto, cut into
  ¼-inch dice
1 4-ounce Spanish chorizo sausage

1½ cups cooked white kidney
  beans (page 63), or use one
  19-ounce can, drained and
  rinsed under water

For *caldo verde*

1 4-ounce Portuguese *chouriço* or
  Spanish chorizo sausage

Heat the olive oil in the pressure cooker over medium-high heat. Add the onion and garlic and sauté 4 to 5 minutes, or until soft. Stir frequently so that the onion does not brown. If making *caldo gallego,* add the serrano ham or prosciutto and chorizo; for *caldo verde* add the *chouriço* or chorizo. Sauté 2 minutes, stirring frequently. Add the potatoes and sauté 1 minute. Add the water and salt. Stir to mix.

Position the lid on the pressure cooker and lock in place. Raise the heat to high and bring to high pressure. Adjust the heat to stabilize pressure, and cook 3 minutes. Remove from heat and lower the pressure using the cold-water-release method. Open the pressure cooker and stir in the shredded kale.

Reposition the lid and lock in place. Place over high heat and bring to high pressure. Adjust heat to stabilize pressure and cook 3 minutes. Remove from heat and lower pressure using the cold-water-release method. Open the pressure cooker. With the back of a large kitchen spoon, gently mash some of the potatoes against the side of the pot to thicken the soup slightly. Taste and adjust for salt. Add the cooked white kidney beans if preparing *caldo gallego.* Slice the cured sausage into ¼-inch-thick slices before serving the soup.

6 SERVINGS

APPROXIMATE NUTRITIONAL ANALYSIS PER SERVING CALDO GALLEGO

298 calories, 13g protein, 32g carbohydrates, 13g fat, 20mg cholesterol, 907mg sodium

APPROXIMATE NUTRITIONAL ANALYSIS PER SERVING CALDO VERDE

185 calories, 6g protein, 16g carbohydrates, 13mg fat, 13mg cholesterol, 731mg sodium

VEGETABLE SOUP WITH BASIL
Soupe au Pistou

This garlicky vegetable-and-bean soup from Provence showcases the exquisite produce of this Mediterranean region of France. The cooking of Provence, especially that of Nice, shares many common variables with neighboring Italy. In fact, *pistou*, which is Niçois for pesto, also means pounded. It is a fresh sauce made with basil that is traditionally crushed with other ingredients with a mortar and pestle. While Italians serve pesto tossed with pasta, the Niçois serve it mixed into this hearty soup, which when enjoyed with a loaf of crusty bread, can easily be a meal in itself.

2 tablespoons olive oil
1 medium onion, finely chopped
1 cup cooked navy beans (page 63)
    or fresh cranberry beans
2 medium potatoes, peeled and
    cut into ¹/₂-inch dice
1 stalk celery, cut into ¹/₄-inch dice
1 medium carrot, peeled, cut into
    ¹/₄-inch dice
8 ounces green beans, trimmed
    and cut into ¹/₂-inch-long pieces
1 leek, white and light green parts
    only, washed well and very
    thinly sliced

2 vine-ripened plum tomatoes,
    peeled, seeded, and finely
    chopped, or 2 canned plum
    tomatoes, seeded and chopped
6 cups water
2 teaspoons salt
¹/₈ teaspoon freshly ground black
    pepper
¹/₂ cup very thin soup noodles or
    vermicelli, broken into 1-inch
    lengths
Freshly grated Parmesan cheese
    for serving

Pistou:

2 cloves garlic, peeled
¹/₂ cup basil leaves, packed,
    washed, and patted dry
4 tablespoons extra-virgin olive oil

Heat the olive oil in the pressure cooker over medium-high heat. Add the onion and sauté 4 to 5 minutes, or until soft. Stir frequently so that the onion does not brown. Add the beans, potato, celery, carrot, green beans, leek, and tomatoes. Cook over high heat for 3 minutes, stirring constantly. Add the water, salt, and black pepper. Position the lid and lock in place. Place over high heat and bring to high pressure. Adjust heat to stabilize pressure and cook 3 minutes. Remove from heat and lower the pressure using the cold-water-release method. Open the pressure cooker. Taste and adjust for salt and pepper.

Prepare the pistou. Place the garlic, basil leaves, olive oil, and 2 tablespoons of the soup in a blender jar. Blend just until mixture is finely chopped and slightly thickened. Set aside

Place the pressure cooker, uncovered, on the burner and bring the soup to a boil. Add the noodles or vermicelli and cook at a simmer until *al dente,* stirring occasionally. Stir in the pistou. Serve with the grated Parmesan cheese.

6 SERVINGS

APPROXIMATE NUTRITIONAL ANALYSIS PER SERVING

280 calories, 6g protein, 34g carbohydrates, 14g fat, 0mg cholesterol, 741mg sodium

VEGETABLE SOUP WITH PASTA
Minestrone

This thick vegetable soup is probably the best known of all Italian soups. It traditionally requires up to three hours of slow simmering, but the use of a pressure cooker cuts the cooking time to under 45 minutes. The addition of a piece of Parmesan cheese rind adds richness and flavor to the soup.

3 tablespoons olive oil
1 medium onion, peeled, minced
3 cloves garlic, peeled, minced
1 tablespoon minced parsley
1 tablespoon minced basil
2 sage leaves, minced
1 cup canned crushed tomatoes
4 teaspoons salt
1/4 teaspoon freshly ground black
   pepper
1 cup diced carrots (1/4-inch dice)
1 cup diced celery (1/4-inch dice)
1 cup diced zucchini (1/4-inch dice)
1 cup diced potatoes (1/4-inch dice)
1 cup 1/2-inch-long pieces string
   bean

8 cups water
Rind from a 1-pound piece of
   Parmesan cheese, wiped clean
   (optional)
2 cups shredded green or Savoy
   cabbage
1 cup cooked red kidney beans
   (page 63), or one 15-ounce can
   drained and rinsed
1 cup ditali (tube-shaped) pasta,
   cooked *al dente*
Freshly grated Parmesan cheese
   for serving

Heat the olive oil in the pressure cooker over medium-high heat. Add the onion, garlic, and herbs and sauté 6 to 8 minutes, stirring frequently so that the mixture does not brown.

Add the tomatoes, salt, and black pepper. Cook 6 minutes, stirring frequently. Add the vegetables, with the exception of the cabbage and beans, mixing well after each addition. Cook 5 minutes, stirring frequently. Add the water and the Parmesan cheese rind, if desired. Mix well.

Position the lid and lock in place. Raise the heat to high and bring to high pressure. Adjust heat to stabilize pressure and cook 10 minutes. Remove from heat and lower the pressure using the cold-water-release method. Open the pressure cooker. Stir in the cabbage and beans.

Reposition the lid on the pressure cooker and lock in place. Over high heat, bring the pressure cooker to high pressure. Adjust heat to stabilize pressure and cook 1 minute. Remove from heat and lower the pressure using the cold-water-release method. Open the pressure cooker. Taste and adjust for salt. Remove and discard the cheese rind. Stir in the pasta. Serve with the grated Parmesan cheese.

8 SERVINGS

APPROXIMATE NUTRITIONAL ANALYSIS PER SERVING

192 calories, 6g protein, 29g carbohydrates, 7g fat, 2mg cholesterol, 1190mg sodium

DRIED BEANS, LEGUMES, AND GRAINS

Dried beans and legumes have always played an important role in the Mediterranean diet. From Portugal in the west to Turkey in the east, beans have sustained the people of the Mediterranean since the days of the ancient Romans, who enjoyed black-eyed peas from Africa and lentils from Egypt. The discovery of the Americas and subsequent trade resulted in the incredible variety of beans that make up the diet in that region today.

The most commonly eaten bean throughout the Mediterranean is the *phaseolus vulgaris*, the common white kidney bean. Chickpeas and lentils are also quite popular and are combined with other ingredients to make spreads, salads, soups, and stews.

A pressure cooker makes the task of preparing dried beans simple and convenient, reducing the cooking time from well over an hour to a matter of minutes. When preparing dried beans and legumes, always inspect them well and remove any foreign matter like small pebbles or twigs. Then rinse them well under cold water in a colander.

To help speed up the cooking process, soak beans in a large bowl of boiling water for one hour, which helps to hydrate them. This step is unnecessary when preparing legumes like lentils or split peas.

Never add salt to beans during the initial cooking, since it toughens the bean skin. Salt should be added along with the remaining ingredients in the recipe once the beans are cooked and tender.

As you will see in some of the bean recipes, when I cook beans I like to add a bay leaf and an onion stuck with cloves for added flavor. This can be eliminated, if desired, but I think that you will agree that the added subtle flavor is worth the small extra effort.

COOKING DRIED BEANS, LEGUMES, AND GRAINS IN A PRESSURE COOKER

The following cooking times are provided as guidelines to be used in cooking dried beans, legumes, and grains in the pressure cooker. Cooking times can vary, depending on the quality and size of these ingredients; maximum and minimum cooking times are given in some instances. When uncertain as to how long to cook something, always start with the shortest cooking time—you can always continue cooking for an additional couple of minutes until the desired texture is reached.

Since water and liquids boil more slowly at an altitude of 2,000 feet above sea level, the cooking time and the amount of cooking liquid needed must be increased accordingly. Please refer to page 28 for additional information.

All cooking times listed begin once high or maximum pressure is reached.

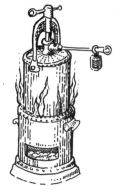

APPROXIMATE COOKING TIMES

DRIED BEANS & LEGUMES	COOKING TIME*	AMOUNT WATER†	YIELD COOKED
Azuki beans, 1 cup dry	9 to 13 minutes	3 cups	2 cups
Black beans, 1 cup dry	13 to 18 minutes	3 cups	2 cups
Black-eyed peas, 1 cup dry	9 to 11 minutes	3 cups	2¼ cups
Chickpeas (garbanzos), 1 cup dry	20 to 25 minutes	3 cups	2½ cups
Cranberry beans, 1 cup dry	20 to 25 minutes	3 cups	2¼ cups
Flageolets, 1 cup dry	10 to 12 minutes	3 cups	2 cups
Gandules (pigeon peas), 1 cup dry	15 to 17 minutes	3 cups	3 cups
Great Northern beans, 1 cup dry	12 to 14 minutes	3 cups	2¼ cups
Kidney beans, red or white, 1 cup dry	12 to 15 minutes	3 cups	2 cups
Lentils, green, brown, or red, 1 cup dry	8 to 10 minutes	3 cups	2 cups
Lima beans, 1 cup dry	8 to 10 minutes	3 cups	2½ cups
Navy or pea beans, 1 cup dry	10 to 12 minutes	3 cups	2 cups
Peas, split green or yellow, 1 cup dry	8 to 10 minutes	3 cups	2 cups
Pinto beans, 1 cup dry	4 to 6 minutes	3 cups	2¼ cups

All beans and dried legumes, with the exception of lentils and split peas, should soak before cooking. Place them in a large bowl, pour boiling water over them, cover with a plate, and let soak one hour. The actual cooking times will vary depending on how old the beans are.

† *Never add salt to beans during the initial cooking. It toughens the bean skin.*

GRAINS	COOKING TIME*	AMOUNT WATER	YIELD COOKED
Barley, pearl, 1 cup dry	15 to 20 minutes	4½ cups	3½ cups
Rice, basmati, 1 cup dry	5 to 7 minutes	1½ cups	3 cups
Rice, Converted or long grain, 1 cup dry	5 to 7 minutes	1½ cups	3 cups
Rice, brown, 1 cup dry	15 to 20 minutes	1¾ cups	2¼ cups
Rice, wild, 1 cup dry	22 to 25 minutes	3 cups	2¼ cups
Wheatberries, 1 cup dry	15 minutes	3 cups	2½ cups

The actual cooking times will vary depending on how old the grain is.

WHITE BEAN PUREE WITH WILTED GREENS
Fagioli alla Campagnola

After winter rains and the arrival of spring, there is a wonderful proliferation of wild greens and herbs in the Italian countryside. Tender young dandelions, watercress, and other greens that we take for common weeds are highly appreciated and welcomed by Italian cooks, who add these offerings from nature to salads and soups.

The following recipe is an adaption of a popular Tuscan country dish of white beans with wild greens sautéed in extra-virgin olive oil with garlic. The contrast of the soft beans and the quickly sautéed, crisp greens makes for an interesting pairing of textures. Serve warm as an appetizer with crusty slices of country bread or as a side dish with roasted meats or poultry.

1 cup dried white kidney beans	1 pound escarole, spinach, chicory,
4 cups boiling water	broccoli di rape, tender
6 cups water	dandelion greens, or any
1 medium onion, peeled and stuck	combination, cleaned, washed,
with 4 whole cloves	dried, and torn into small pieces
1 bay leaf	Salt
3 tablespoons extra-virgin olive oil	Freshly ground black pepper
3 cloves garlic, peeled and minced	Extra-virgin olive oil for serving

Rinse the kidney beans in a colander under cold water. Place in a large, heatproof bowl and cover with boiling water. Cover with a plate and let soak 1 hour.

Drain the soaked beans and place in the pressure cooker with the water, onion, and bay leaf. Position the lid and lock in place. Place over high heat and bring to high pressure. Adjust the heat to stabilize the pressure and cook 15 minutes. Remove from the heat and lower the pressure using the cold-water-release method. Open the pressure cooker. If the beans are not tender, lock the lid in place and cook an additional 2 to 3 minutes, or until tender, under high pressure.

Remove and discard the onion and bay leaf. Drain the cooked beans, reserving ½ cup of the cooked liquid. Rinse and dry the pressure cooker. Add the olive oil and garlic to the pressure cooker. Over medium-high heat, sauté the garlic just until it begins to brown. Add the greens immediately and cook just until wilted. Add the cooked kidney beans and 2 tablespoons of the reserved liquid. Stir well. When the mixture is heated through, gently mash with a potato masher or the back of a large slotted spoon, adding additional liquid so that the mixture has the consistency of soft mashed potatoes. Do not overmash. Season with salt and black pepper to taste. Mound on a serving dish and drizzle with olive oil.

4 SERVINGS

APPROXIMATE NUTRITIONAL ANALYSIS PER SERVING

294 calories, 10g protein, 34g carbohydrates, 14g fat, 0mg cholesterol, 1097mg sodium

WARM SHRIMP AND BEAN SALAD

I will admit that in my travels to the Mediterranean I have never been served this dish, which combines two of my favorite foods: shrimp and beans. I must say, however, that the combination is sublime. Try serving it as a lunch entrée or as a light supper.

2 cups dried white kidney beans
6 cups boiling water
8 cups water
1 large onion, peeled and stuck
    with 6 whole cloves
1 bay leaf
8 tablespoons extra-virgin olive oil
Juice of one lime
2 cloves garlic, peeled and minced
4 scallions, trimmed, white and
    green parts sliced thin
1/4 cup minced parsley
1/4 cup minced cilantro,
    1 tablespoon reserved for
    garnish
1/2 teaspoon ground cumin

2 teaspoons salt
1/8 teaspoon freshly ground black
    pepper
1/2 red pepper, seeded and cut into
    1/4-inch dice
1/2 yellow pepper, seeded and cut
    into 1/4-inch dice
2 cups Rich Vegetable Stock (page
    46) or canned vegetable broth
1/2 cup dry white wine
1 bay leaf
1 pound large shrimp, peeled and
    deveined, with tails intact,
    rinsed under cold water

Rinse the kidney beans in a colander under cold water. Place in a large, heatproof bowl and cover with boiling water. Cover with a plate and let soak 1 hour.

Drain the soaked beans and place in the pressure cooker with the water, onion, and bay leaf. Position the lid and lock in place. Place over high heat and bring to high pressure. Adjust the heat to stabilize the pressure and cook 15 minutes. Remove from heat and lower pressure using the cold-water-release method. Open the pressure cooker. If the beans are not tender, lock the lid in position and cook an additional 2 to 3 minutes under high pressure. Drain the cooked beans, reserving 1/4 cup of the cooking liquid.

Prepare the vinaigrette by whisking the reserved cooking liquid, olive oil, lime juice, garlic, scallions, parsley, cilantro, cumin, salt, and black pepper in a large bowl.

Add the white beans and the diced red and yellow pepper. Toss gently. Taste and adjust for salt and pepper. Cover and set aside.

Place the stock, white wine, and bay leaf in a medium-sized saucepan and bring to a boil over high heat. Add the cleaned shrimp. When the cooking liquid begins to boil again, lower the heat to a simmer. Cook the shrimp 2 to 3 minutes, or just until cooked. Remove with a slotted spoon to a strainer.

Spoon the bean salad onto a large serving platter. Arrange the cooked shrimp on top. Sprinkle with the reserved tablespoon of cilantro.

4 SERVINGS

APPROXIMATE NUTRITIONAL ANALYSIS PER SERVING

735 calories, 42g protein, 70g carbohydrates, 31g fat, 175mg cholesterol, 1484mg sodium

WHITE BEAN SALAD
Piyaz

This white-bean salad from Turkey is a wonderful departure from our standard potato salads and cole slaws of summer. Serve it at your next barbecue or picnic.

2 cups navy beans
4 cups boiling water
1 medium onion, peeled and stuck
  with 4 whole, dried cloves
1 bay leaf
6 cups water
4 tablespoons extra-virgin olive oil
4 tablespoons freshly squeezed
  lemon juice
1 tablespoon white-wine vinegar
1 clove garlic, peeled and minced

¹/₄ cup finely chopped parsley
1 teaspoon finely chopped mint
2 teaspoons snipped dill
1 small red onion, cut in half and
  thinly sliced
1 teaspoon salt
1 green pepper, cored, seeded, and
  sliced into thin rings
2 hard-boiled eggs, shelled and
  quartered

Rinse the navy beans in a colander under cold water. Place in a large heatproof bowl and cover with boiling water. Cover with a plate and let soak 1 hour.

Drain the soaked beans and place in the pressure cooker with the onion, bay leaf, and cold water. Position the lid and lock in place. Place over high heat and bring to high pressure. Adjust heat to stabilize pressure and cook 12 minutes. Remove from heat and lower pressure using the cold-water-release method. If the beans are not tender, lock the lid in position and cook an additional 2 to 3 minutes, or until tender, under high pressure.

Remove from the heat and lower the pressure using the cold-water-release method. Open the pressure cooker. Remove and discard the onion and bay leaf. Drain the beans in a large colander.

Prepare the vinaigrette by whisking the olive oil, lemon juice, vinegar, garlic, parsley, mint, and dill in a large serving bowl. Add the hot cooked beans and sliced onion. Toss gently to combine. Let cool to room temperature. Taste and adjust for salt. Garnish with the sliced green pepper and hard-boiled eggs.

6 SERVINGS

APPROXIMATE NUTRITIONAL ANALYSIS PER SERVING

214 calories, 8g protein, 21g carbohydrates, 11g fat, 71mg cholesterol, 386mg sodium

GREEK BEAN SOUP
Fassolatha

This tomato-rich Greek bean soup is simple and quick to prepare when using a pressure cooker. Serve it as they would in Greece, with a good loaf of bread, a piece of cheese, and some sun-ripened fruit, for a complete meal.

2 cups white kidney beans	1 ½ cups canned crushed
4 cups boiling water	tomatoes
4 tablespoons olive oil	1 bay leaf
1 large onion, finely chopped	5 cups water
2 cloves garlic, peeled and minced	Salt to taste
2 large carrots, peeled and cut into	Freshly ground black pepper to
¼-inch dice	taste
4 stalks celery, cut into ¼-inch dice	4 tablespoons minced parsley

Rinse the kidney beans in a colander under cold water. Place in a large, heatproof bowl and cover with the boiling water. Cover with a plate and let soak 1 hour.

Heat the olive oil in the pressure cooker over medium-high heat. Add the onion and garlic and sauté 4 to 5 minutes, or until soft. Stir frequently so that the onion does not brown. Add the carrots and celery and sauté 2 minutes. Add the tomatoes and sauté 2 minutes, stirring frequently.

Drain the soaked beans and add to the vegetable mixture. Stir well. Pour in the water. Position the lid and lock in place. Raise heat to high and bring to high pressure. Adjust the heat to stabilize the pressure and cook 15 minutes. Remove from the heat and lower the pressure using the cold-water-release method. Open the pressure cooker. If the beans are not tender, lock the lid in position and cook an additional 2 to 3 minutes, or until tender, under high pressure.

Remove from the heat and lower the pressure using the cold-water-release method. Open the pressure cooker. Remove the bay leaf. With the back of a large spoon, mash some of the beans against the side of the pot to thicken the soup, if desired. Season with salt and black pepper to taste. Stir in the minced parsley before serving.

6 SERVINGS

APPROXIMATE NUTRITIONAL ANALYSIS PER SERVING

448 calories, 20g protein, 72g carbohydrates, 10g fat, 0mg cholesterol, 852mg sodium

TURKISH BEAN STEW
Fasulye Plakisi

Although they have been political and military rivals for centuries, Turkey and Greece share many culinary influences. At first glance, this recipe may appear similar to that for the Greek bean soup; however, at closer inspection you will notice the addition of lemon juice and the thicker, stewlike consistency of the dish.

2 cups white kidney beans
4 cups boiling water
4 tablespoons olive oil
2 large onions, finely chopped
2 cloves garlic, peeled and minced
3 large carrots, peeled and cut into
    $^{1}/_{4}$-inch dice
3 stalks celery, cut into $^{1}/_{4}$-inch dice
$^{1}/_{2}$ cup canned crushed tomatoes

Pinch cayenne pepper
5 cups water
Salt to taste
Freshly ground black pepper to
    taste
2 tablespoons freshly squeezed
    lemon juice
$^{1}/_{4}$ cup finely minced parsley

Rinse the kidney beans in a colander under cold water. Place in a large, heatproof bowl and cover with the boiling water. Cover with a plate and let soak 1 hour.

Heat the olive oil in the pressure cooker over medium-high heat. Add the onion and garlic and sauté 4 to 5 minutes, or until the onion is soft. Stir frequently so that the onion does not brown. Add the carrots and celery and sauté 2 minutes. Add the tomatoes and cayenne pepper and sauté 2 minutes, stirring frequently.

Drain the soaked beans and add to the vegetable mixture in the pressure cooker. Stir well. Add the water. Position the lid and lock in place. Heat to high and bring to high pressure. Adjust heat to stabilize the pressure and cook 15 minutes. Remove from the heat and lower the pressure using the cold-water-release method. Open the pressure cooker. If the beans are not tender, lock the lid in position and cook an additional 2 to 3 minutes, or until tender, under high pressure. Remove from the heat and lower pressure using the cold-water-release method.

Open the pressure cooker. Season with salt and black pepper to taste. Stir in the lemon juice and simmer, uncovered, 5 minutes. Sprinkle with parsley before serving.

6 SERVINGS

APPROXIMATE NUTRITIONAL ANALYSIS PER SERVING

457 calories, 20g protein, 74g carbohydrates, 10g fat, 0mg cholesterol, 787mg sodium

SPANISH BEAN SOUP
Potaje de Alubias

Cured pork products like *chorizo* and ham are commonplace in many dishes from the Iberian Peninsula, especially in bean-based soups, where they add delicious flavor and character.

Potaje is a typical Spanish soup made from beans, lentils, or chickpeas, and it is served in most Spanish homes at least once a week, if not more.

2 cups white kidney beans
4 cups boiling water
3 tablespoons olive oil
1 large onion, finely chopped
3 cloves garlic, peeled and minced
1/2 green pepper, finely chopped
4 tablespoons canned crushed
  tomatoes

1 teaspoon paprika
5 cups cold water
1 bay leaf
Salt to taste
Freshly ground black pepper to
  taste

Optional ingredients:

2 small, cured chorizo sausages,
  cut into 1-inch pieces
2 medium-sized potatoes, peeled
  and cut into 1/2-inch dice

1 1/2 pounds Swiss chard, thick
  stems removed, coarsely
  chopped

Rinse the kidney beans in a colander under cold water. Place in a large, heatproof bowl and cover with the boiling water. Cover with a plate and let soak 1 hour.

Heat the olive oil in the pressure cooker over medium-high heat. Add the onion, garlic, green pepper, and tomatoes and sauté 6 to 8 minutes, or until soft and thick. Stir frequently so that the mixture does not brown. Add the paprika and sauté 1 minute longer.

Drain the soaked kidney beans and add to the pressure cooker. Stir well. Pour in the water and add the bay leaf and the optional chorizo and/or potatoes. Place the lid and lock in position. Raise the heat to high and bring to high pressure. Adjust heat to stabilize pressure, and cook 15 minutes. Remove from the heat and lower the pressure using the cold-water-release method. Open the pressure cooker. If the beans are not tender, lock the lid in position and cook an additional 2 to 3 minutes, or until tender, under high pressure.

Remove from heat and lower pressure using the cold-water-release method. If you wish to add the chopped Swiss chard, do so now. Reposition the lid on the pressure cooker and cook under high pressure 2 minutes. Remove from the heat and release the pressure using the cold-water-release method. Open the pressure cooker. Season with salt and black pepper to taste.

6 SERVINGS

APPROXIMATE NUTRITIONAL ANALYSIS PER SERVING WITH OPTIONAL CHORIZO, POTATOES, AND SWISS CHARD

561 calories, 27g protein, 81g carbohydrates, 16g fat, 18mg cholesterol, 1233mg sodium

MACARONI AND BEANS
Pasta e Fagioli

Pasta e fagioli is comfort food that someone's mother or grandmother would prepare at home for her family. Ironically, as home-style cooking has become more popular at Italian restaurants, this very humble, basic dish appears on the menus of even the most elite restaurants.

1 cup white kidney beans
4 cups boiling water
2 tablespoons olive oil
1 small onion, finely chopped
1 clove garlic, peeled and minced
1 slice pancetta or unsmoked bacon, finely chopped
1 fresh or canned plum tomato, peeled, seeded, and finely chopped
1 small carrot, peeled and cut into ¼-inch dice
1 stalk celery, cut into ¼-inch dice
2 fresh sage leaves, minced, or ¼ teaspoon dried

3 cups Rich Chicken Stock (page 47), Rich Beef Stock (page 48), Rich Vegetable Stock (page 46), or canned broth
1 cup water
Salt to taste
Freshly ground black pepper to taste
2 cups ditali or small shell pasta, cooked *al dente*
Extra-virgin olive oil for drizzling
Freshly grated Pecorino Romano cheese for serving

Rinse the kidney beans in a colander under cold water. Place in a large heatproof bowl and cover with boiling water. Cover with a plate and let soak 1 hour.

Heat the olive oil in the pressure cooker over medium-high heat. Add the onion, garlic, and pancetta and sauté 4 to 5 minutes, or until the onion is soft. Stir frequently so that the mixture does not brown. Add the tomato, carrot, celery, and sage. Sauté 2 minutes, stirring frequently. Drain the soaked kidney beans and add to the vegetable mixture. Add the stock and water. Stir well.

Place the lid and lock in position. Raise the heat to high and bring to high pressure. Adjust the heat to stabilize the pressure and cook 15 minutes. Remove from heat and lower pressure using the cold-water-release method. Open the pressure cooker. If the beans are not tender, lock the lid in position and cook an additional 2 to 3 minutes, or until tender, under high pressure.

Open the pressure cooker. Season with salt and black pepper to taste. Add the cooked pasta to the soup. Drizzle each serving with a teaspoon of extra-virgin olive oil. Serve with grated Pecorino Romano cheese.

4 SERVINGS

APPROXIMATE NUTRITIONAL ANALYSIS PER SERVING

529 calories, 29g protein, 70g carbohydrates, 16g fat, 7mg cholesterol, 2586mg sodium

NORTH AFRICAN CHICKPEA SALAD

MOROCCO, ALGERIA, AND TUNISIA

This North African salad combines two of the oldest ingredients used in the region, chickpeas and cilantro, which have played an important role in the diet of the inhabitants of the Mediterranean basin since the beginning of written history. Serve this refreshing salad as a light lunch with marinated tuna steaks (page 137) or as an accompaniment to any of the other North African dishes in this book.

1 cup dried chickpeas
4 cups boiling water
4 cups cold water
1 medium onion, peeled and stuck
    with 4 whole cloves
1 bay leaf
3 tablespoons olive oil
3 tablespoons freshly squeezed
    lemon juice
1 clove garlic, peeled and minced

1/2 teaspoon ground cumin
1 teaspoon salt
1/8 teaspoon freshly ground black
    pepper
1 small red onion, peeled, cut in
    half and thinly sliced
1 large, ripe tomato, seeded and
    diced
2 tablespoons minced cilantro

Rinse the chickpeas in a colander under cold water. Place in a large, heatproof bowl and cover with the boiling water. Cover with a plate and let soak 1 hour.

Drain the soaked chickpeas and place in the pressure cooker with the water, onion, and bay leaf.

Position the lid and lock in place. Place over high heat and bring to high pressure. Adjust heat to stabilize pressure and cook 25 minutes. Remove from heat and lower pressure using the cold-water-release method. If the chickpeas are not tender, lock the lid in position and cook an additional 2 to 3 minutes, or until tender, under high pressure.

Remove and discard the onion and bay leaf. Drain the chickpeas in a large colander. Let cool to room temperature.

Prepare the vinaigrette by whisking together the olive oil, lemon juice, garlic, cumin, salt, and black pepper. Add the cooked chickpeas, onion, tomato, and cilantro and toss well. Cover and let sit at room temperature at least 1 hour before serving.

4 SERVINGS

APPROXIMATE NUTRITIONAL ANALYSIS PER SERVING

304 calories, 11g protein, 38g carbohydrates, 14g fat, 0mg cholesterol, 555mg sodium

CHICKPEA SPREAD
Humus

GREECE, LEBANON, JORDAN, AND SYRIA ·

Humus—a thick, eastern Mediterranean and Middle Eastern spread made from mashed chickpeas seasoned with lemon juice, garlic, and olive oil—is usually served as an appetizer with pieces of pita bread. Chickpeas, which are high in protein (9 grams per $1/2$ cup serving), have only 3 grams of fat and less than 1 gram of saturated fat, making humus an excellent snack for those watching their fat intake. Furthermore, the addition of parsley, another Mediterranean staple, provides 43 percent of the recommended daily allowance of vitamin C.

1 cup dried chickpeas
4 cups boiling water
4 cups cold water
1 medium onion, peeled and
   stuck with 4 whole
   cloves
1 bay leaf
2 cloves garlic, peeled and
   chopped

$1/2$ cup parsley leaves, washed,
   well-dried, and packed
3 tablespoons freshly squeezed
   lemon juice
1 teaspoon salt
$1/4$ cup plus 1 tablespoon
   extra-virgin olive oil

Rinse the chickpeas in a colander under cold water. Place in a large, heatproof bowl and cover with boiling water. Cover with a plate and let soak 1 hour.

Drain the soaked chickpeas and place in the pressure cooker with the cold water, onion, and bay leaf. Position the lid and lock in place. Place over high heat and bring to maximum pressure. Adjust the heat to stabilize the pressure and cook 25 minutes. Remove from the heat and lower the pressure using the cold-water-release method. If the chickpeas are not tender, lock the lid in position and cook an additional 2 to 3 minutes, or until tender, under high pressure.

Remove and discard the onion and bay leaf. Drain the chickpeas in a large colander, reserving $1/4$ cup of the cooking liquid.

In a food processor, blend the cooked chickpeas and all the remaining ingredients, except the olive oil, until chickpeas are mashed. With the food processor running, slowly add $1/4$ cup of the olive oil through the feed tube. Add some of the reserved cooking liquid if necessary—the chickpea spread should have the consistency of mashed potatoes. Taste and adjust for salt. Spoon the mixture into a serving bowl. Drizzle with the remaining olive oil. Serve with crudités or toasted pita-bread triangles.

6 SERVINGS

APPROXIMATE NUTRITIONAL ANALYSIS PER SERVING

233 calories, 7g protein, 23g carbohydrates, 13g fat, 0mg cholesterol, 367mg sodium

CHICKPEAS WITH SPINACH
Garbanzos con Espinacas

Chickpeas, or garbanzos, used to be referred to in Spain as *la carne de los pobres*—poor man's meat—since they were readily available to even the poorest of the poor as a vital source of protein. In addition to being used in spreads, soups, and stews, garbanzos are also toasted until crunchy and eaten as a snack food, a custom that can be traced back to the early Middle Ages, when Spain prospered under 700 years of Moorish rule.

The following recipe for chickpeas with spinach is served in homes throughout Spain as a first course or at neighborhood bars and cafés as a tapa to accompany a glass of wine or beer. This dish is especially popular during the meatless days of Lent, when salted codfish may also be added, turning this dish into a complete one-pot meal.

2 cups chickpeas
4 cups boiling water
6 cups water
1 large onion, peeled and stuck
   with 6 whole cloves
1 bay leaf
3 tablespoons olive oil
1 large onion, finely chopped
3 cloves garlic, peeled and minced
1 small green pepper, seeded and
   finely chopped

6 tablespoons canned crushed
   tomatoes
1 tablespoon paprika
$\frac{1}{2}$ teaspoon dried cumin
3 teaspoons salt
$\frac{1}{8}$ teaspoon freshly ground black
   pepper
5 threads of saffron (optional)
1 pound spinach, trimmed,
   washed well to remove all grit,
   and coarsely chopped

Rinse the chickpeas in a colander under cold water. Place in a large, heatproof bowl and cover with boiling water. Cover with a plate and let soak 1 hour.

Drain the soaked chickpeas and place in the pressure cooker with the water, onion, and bay leaf. Position the lid and lock in place. Place over high heat and bring to high pressure. Adjust the heat to stabilize the pressure and cook 25 minutes. Remove from the heat and lower the pressure using the cold-water-release method. Open the pressure cooker. If the chickpeas are not tender, lock the lid in position and cook an additional 4 to 5 minutes, or until tender, under high pressure. Open the pressure cooker, remove and discard the onion and bay leaf. Ladle out and discard 1 cup of the cooking liquid.

While the chickpeas are cooking, heat the olive oil in a medium-sized skillet over medium-high heat. Prepare a sofrito by sautéing the onion, garlic, green pepper, and tomatoes 6 to 8 minutes, or until the vegetables are soft and the mixture is thick. Stir frequently so that the sofrito does not burn. Stir in the paprika, the cumin, 1 teaspoon of the salt, the black pepper, and the saffron, if desired, and cook 1 minute.

Add the sofrito to the cooked chickpeas in the pressure cooker, along with the remaining 2 teaspoons salt and the spinach. Stir well to blend. Position the lid on the pressure cooker and lock in place. Raise the heat to high and bring to high pressure. Adjust the heat to stabilize the pressure and cook 2 minutes. Remove from the heat and lower the pressure using the cold-water-release method. Open the pressure cooker. Taste and adjust for salt.

4 SERVINGS

APPROXIMATE NUTRITIONAL ANALYSIS PER SERVING

467 calories, 24g protein, 75g carbohydrates, 10g fat, 0mg cholesterol, 1762mg sodium

LENTIL SALAD

While lentils appear in many different guises in Mediterranean cooking, I have never seen them served in a salad. This is unfortunate, since tiny lentils combine so well with a vinaigrette and freshly minced herbs as in this Mediterranean-inspired salad.

2 cups lentils
5 cups cold water
1 large onion, peeled and stuck
   with 6 whole cloves
1 bay leaf
4 tablespoons extra-virgin olive oil
3 tablespoons white-wine vinegar
3 tablespoons finely chopped fresh
   herbs, such as tarragon, parsley,
   or basil, or any combination

1 clove garlic, peeled and minced
1 teaspoon salt
1/8 teaspoon freshly ground black
   pepper
2 scallions, trimmed, white and
   light green parts sliced thin
2 vine-ripened plum tomatoes,
   peeled, seeded, and diced
1/4 cup crumbled feta cheese
   (optional)

Rinse the lentils in a colander under cold water. Place in the pressure cooker with the cold water, onion, and bay leaf. Position the lid and lock in place. Place over high heat and bring to high pressure. Adjust the heat to stabilize the pressure and cook 8 minutes. Remove from heat and lower pressure using the cold-water-release method. Open the pressure cooker. If the lentils are not tender, lock the lid in position and cook an additional 1 to 2 minutes, or until tender, under high pressure. Open the pressure cooker and discard the onion and bay leaf. Drain the cooked lentils and place them in a serving bowl.

Prepare the vinaigrette by whisking together the olive oil, vinegar, herbs, garlic, salt, and black pepper. Pour the vinaigrette over the warm lentils and toss well. Let sit at room temperature 1 hour. Add the chopped scallions and tomatoes before serving. Taste and adjust for salt. Sprinkle with the crumbled feta cheese, if desired.

4 SERVINGS

APPROXIMATE NUTRITIONAL ANALYSIS PER SERVING WITH FETA CHEESE
493 calories, 29g protein, 62g carbohydrates, 16g fat, 6mg cholesterol, 630mg sodium

PASTA AND LENTILS
Pasta e Lenticchie

ITALY

Having grown up in an Italian-Catholic household, I remember the days of meatless Fridays, when my mother would prepare soups made with dried legumes or vegetables to which she would add pasta and extra-virgin olive oil. While we never gave these meals much thought, it is now clear that the ingredients—lentils, beans, leafy greens and vegetables, pasta, and olive oil—all fundamental components of the Mediterranean Diet, provide superior nutritional value. In fact, $1/2$ cup of cooked lentils, which contains no cholesterol and only 1 gram of fat and saturated fat, provides 9 grams of protein.

2 cups lentils
2 tablespoons olive oil
1 medium onion, finely chopped
2 medium carrots, peeled and cut into $1/4$-inch dice
1 stalk celery, cut into $1/4$-inch dice
2 canned plum tomatoes, seeded and finely chopped
3 cloves garlic, peeled and crushed
1 bay leaf

6 cups water
1 cup small tubular pasta like ditalini or tubetti, cooked *al dente*
Salt and pepper to taste
Extra-virgin olive oil for drizzling (optional)
Freshly grated Pecorino Romano cheese (optional)

Place the lentils in a large colander. Rinse well under cold water and set aside.

Heat the olive oil in the pressure cooker over medium heat. Add the onion and sauté 4 to 5 minutes, or until soft. Stir frequently so that the onion does not brown. Add the diced carrots, celery, and chopped tomatoes. Cook 2 minutes, stirring frequently. Add the lentils, garlic, bay leaf, and water. Stir to blend.

Position the lid and lock in place. Raise the heat to high and bring to high pressure. Adjust the heat to stabilize the pressure and cook 10 minutes. Remove from the heat and lower the pressure using the cold-water-release method. Open the pressure cooker. Test the lentils to see if they are tender. If not, lock the lid in place and cook an additional 1 to 2 minutes under high pressure.

When the lentils are tender, mash the softened garlic cloves by pressing them against the side of the pot with the back of a spoon. Taste and adjust for salt (up to 3 teaspoons) and pepper (about $1/4$ teaspoon). Stir in the cooked pasta. If desired, drizzle

DRIED BEANS, LEGUMES, AND GRAINS   81

each plate of lentils with a teaspoon of extra-virgin olive oil and serve with grated Pecorino Romano cheese.

4 SERVINGS

APPROXIMATE NUTRITIONAL ANALYSIS PER SERVING

475 calories, 30g protein, 68g carbohydrates, 12g fat, 0mg cholesterol, 1640mg sodium

RISOTTO

Creamy risotto is traditionally a time- and labor-intensive Italian rice dish. The cook slowly adds the cooking liquid to the rice, stirring almost constantly. The following pressure-cooker method may not be traditional, but the results are excellent, and the method is much simpler and less time-consuming. Once it is ready, risotto must be served straight from the pot—otherwise it will thicken and become pasty. Risotto is traditionally served in Italy as a first course, and this recipe is the classic.

Risotto with Parmesan Cheese
- ◆ *Risotto in Bianco, Italy*

3 tablespoons unsalted butter
1 small onion, finely chopped
1 cup Italian arborio or other
   short-grain rice
2 ¼ cups Rich Chicken Stock
   (page 47), Rich Beef Stock (page
   48), Rich Vegetable Stock (page
   46), or canned broth

⅓ cup freshly grated Parmesan
   cheese
⅛ teaspoon ground white pepper

Heat 2 tablespoons of the butter in the pressure cooker over medium-high heat. Add the onion and sauté 4 to 5 minutes, or until soft. Stir frequently so that the onion does not brown. Add the rice and sauté, stirring often, until lightly golden. Pour in the stock. Stir well.

Position the lid and lock in place. Raise the heat to high and bring to high pressure. Adjust the heat to stabilize the pressure and cook 7 minutes. Remove from heat and lower pressure using the cold-water-release method.

Open the pressure cooker. Stir in the remaining tablespoon of butter, the Parmesan, and the white pepper. Let the risotto sit in the pressure cooker until the butter and cheese have melted. Stir one more time and serve at once with additional Parmesan cheese, if desired.

4 SERVINGS

APPROXIMATE NUTRITIONAL ANALYSIS PER SERVING

299 calories, 13g protein, 32g carbohydrates, 13g fat, 31mg cholesterol, 1110mg sodium

RISOTTO WITH MUSHROOMS
Risotto ai Funghi

In this recipe, the rich flavor of dried porcini mushrooms is a wonderful complement to the Parmesan cheese. If you wish, substitute a half cup of fresh wild mushrooms.

¼ cup dried porcini mushrooms
1 cup boiling water
3 tablespoons unsalted butter
1 small onion, finely chopped
1 cup Italian arborio or other
    short-grain rice
¼ cup dry white wine
2 cups Rich Chicken Stock (page
    47), Rich Beef Stock (page 48), or
    Rich Vegetable Stock (page 46),
    or canned broth

⅓ cup freshly grated Parmesan
    cheese
⅛ teaspoon freshly ground white
    pepper

Soak the dried porcini in the boiling water 6 to 8 minutes, or until hydrated. Remove the porcini and coarsely chop.

Heat 2 tablespoons of the butter in the pressure cooker over medium-high heat. Add the onion and sauté 4 to 5 minutes, or until soft. Stir frequently so that the onion does not brown. Add the rice and sauté, stirring often, until lightly golden. Add the white wine, stock, and porcini. Stir well.

Position the lid and lock in place. Raise the heat to high and bring to high pressure. Adjust the heat to stabilize the pressure and cook 7 minutes. Remove from heat and lower pressure using the cold-water-release method.

Open the pressure cooker. Stir in the remaining tablespoon of butter, the Parmesan, and the white pepper. Let the risotto sit in the pressure cooker until the butter and cheese have melted. Stir one more time and serve at once with additional Parmesan, if desired.

4 SERVINGS

APPROXIMATE NUTRITIONAL ANALYSIS PER SERVING
341 calories, 16g protein, 36g carbohydrates, 13g fat, 31mg cholesterol, 1116mg sodium

RISOTTO WITH SPRING VEGETABLES
Risotto alla Primavera

This vegetable-packed risotto is a delicious lunch and can make a complete dinner meal when accompanied by a warm bean dish like White Bean Puree with Wilted Greens (page 64).

2 tablespoons olive oil
1 clove garlic, peeled and minced
1/2 cup shelled fresh or frozen peas
1/4 pound asparagus spears, trimmed and cut into 1-inch lengths
1 small zucchini, trimmed and cut into 1/4-inch dice
2 vine-ripened plum tomatoes, peeled, seeded, and finely chopped, or 2 canned plum tomatoes, seeded and finely chopped

2 1/2 cups Rich Chicken Stock (page 47), Rich Vegetable Stock (page 46), or canned broth
2 tablespoons minced parsley
3 tablespoons unsalted butter
1 small onion, finely chopped
1 cup Italian arborio or other short-grain rice
1/4 cup dry white wine
1/3 cup freshly grated Parmesan cheese
1/8 teaspoon freshly ground black pepper

Heat the olive oil in a medium-sized skillet over medium-high heat. Add the garlic and sauté 30 seconds. Add the vegetables and sauté 5 minutes, stirring frequently. Add 1/2 cup of the stock and cook until the vegetables are tender. Uncover and bring to a boil to reduce the stock. Add the parsley. Remove from heat, cover, and set aside.

Heat 2 tablespoons of the butter in the pressure cooker over medium-high heat. Add the onion and sauté 4 to 5 minutes, or until soft. Stir frequently so that the onion does not brown. Add the rice and sauté, stirring often, until lightly golden. Add the white wine and the remaining 2 cups stock. Stir well.

Position the lid and lock in place. Raise the heat to high and bring to high pressure. Adjust the heat to stabilize the pressure and cook 7 minutes. Remove from the heat and lower the pressure using the cold-water-release method.

Open the pressure cooker. Stir in the sautéed vegetables, the remaining tablespoon of butter, the Parmesan cheese, and the black pepper. Let the risotto sit in the pressure cooker until the butter and cheese have melted. Stir one more time and serve at once with additional Parmesan, if desired.

4 SERVINGS

APPROXIMATE NUTRITIONAL ANALYSIS PER SERVING

398 calories, 15g protein, 38g carbohydrates, 20g fat, 31mg cholesterol, 1118mg sodium

RISOTTO WITH SAFFRON
Risotto alla Milanese

The red wine and saffron in this traditional recipe result in a richly colored risotto.

3 tablespoons unsalted butter
1 small onion, finely chopped
1 cup Italian arborio or other
short-grain rice
1/4 cup dry red wine
6 saffron strands crushed to a
powder
2 cups Rich Chicken Stock (page
47), Rich Beef Stock (page 48), or
Rich Vegetable Stock (page 46),
or canned broth

1/3 cup freshly grated Parmesan
cheese
1/8 teaspoon freshly ground black
pepper

Heat 2 tablespoons of the butter in the pressure cooker over medium-high heat. Add the onion and sauté 4 to 5 minutes, or until soft. Stir frequently so that the onion does not brown. Add the rice and sauté, stirring often, until lightly golden. Add the red wine. Bring to a boil over high heat. Once the alcohol has evaporated, add the saffron and stock.

Position the lid and lock in place. Raise the heat to high and bring to high pressure. Adjust the heat to stabilize the pressure and cook 7 minutes. Remove from the heat and lower the pressure using the cold-water-release method.

Open the pressure cooker. Stir in the remaining tablespoon of butter, the Parmesan, and black pepper. Let the risotto sit in the pressure cooker until the butter and cheese have melted. Stir one more time and serve at once with additional Parmesan, if desired.

4 SERVINGS

APPROXIMATE NUTRITIONAL ANALYSIS PER SERVING

292 calories, 11g protein, 34g carbohydrates, 13g fat, 31mg cholesterol, 872mg sodium

RICE AND PEAS
Risi e Bisi

This Venetian dish is traditionally served on April 25, the feast of St. Mark, the patron saint of Venice. It also coincides with the arrival of the first, tender fresh peas of the season. Frozen peas are a convenient substitute, although the Venetians would probably never consider using them. While neither as thick nor as dry as risotto, *risi e bisi* is, however, much drier than soup, with just enough broth to make it necessary to eat it with a spoon.

3 tablespoons unsalted butter
1 small onion, finely chopped
1 cup fresh or frozen peas
1 cup Italian arborio or other
    short-grain rice
4 cups Rich Chicken Stock (page
    47), Rich Vegetable Stock (page
    46), or canned broth

2 tablespoons minced parsley
1/2 cup freshly grated Parmesan
    cheese

Heat the butter in the pressure cooker over medium-high heat. Add the onion and sauté 4 to 5 minutes, or until soft. Stir frequently so that the onion does not brown. Add the peas and sauté 2 minutes. Add the rice and stock. Stir well.

Position the lid and lock in place. Raise the heat to high and bring to high pressure. Adjust the heat to stabilize the pressure and cook 6 minutes. Remove from the heat and lower the pressure using the cold-water-release method. Open the pressure cooker. Stir in the parsley and Parmesan before serving.

4 SERVINGS

APPROXIMATE NUTRITIONAL ANALYSIS PER SERVING

395 calories, 23g protein, 39g carbohydrates, 16g fat, 36mg cholesterol, 2146mg sodium

BASIC RICE PILAF

Rice pilaf is enjoyed throughout the Arabic countries that border the Mediterranean. Variations on rice pilaf—fluffier than risotto and usually served as an accompaniment to main dishes—are endless and are really only limited by the cook's imagination. The following recipe is a good starting point and serves as an excellent accompaniment to any of the meat and poultry dishes in this cookbook.

2 tablespoons olive oil
2 tablespoons unsalted butter
1 medium onion, chopped
1 clove garlic, peeled and minced
1^1/$_2$ cups long-grain rice

2^1/$_2$ cups Rich Chicken Stock (page 47), Rich Beef Stock (page 48), or Rich Vegetable Stock (page 46), or canned broth

Heat the olive oil and butter in the pressure cooker over medium-high heat. Add the onion and sauté 4 to 5 minutes, or until soft. Stir frequently so that the onion does not brown. Add the garlic and rice. Sauté, stirring constantly 3 to 4 minutes, or until the rice just begins to turn golden. Add the stock and stir well.

Place the lid and lock in place. Raise the heat to high and bring to high pressure. Adjust the heat to stabilize the pressure and cook 6 minutes. Remove from the heat and lower the pressure using the cold-water-release method. Open the pressure cooker. Set the lid on the pressure cooker and let the rice sit 5 minutes. Fluff with a fork before serving.

4 SERVINGS

APPROXIMATE NUTRITIONAL ANALYSIS PER SERVING

447 calories, 13g protein, 64g carbohydrates, 15g fat, 17mg cholesterol, 958mg sodium

YELLOW SPLIT-PEA SPREAD
Fava me Lahanika

♦ *Louvana, Cyprus*

The following recipe for yellow split-pea spread is a taverna favorite in both Greece and Cyprus, where it is part of the *mezethes* (in Greece) or *mezethakia* (in Cyprus), an array of small dishes of appetizers usually enjoyed with ouzo, wine, or beer.

1 cup yellow split peas
7 tablespoons extra-virgin olive oil
1 large onion, finely chopped
3 cloves garlic, peeled and crushed
2 cups water
Salt to taste

Freshly ground black pepper to
  taste
Juice of one large lemon
1 teaspoon capers, rinsed under
  water and drained

Place the split peas in a large colander and rinse well under cold water.

Heat 4 tablespoons of the olive oil in the pressure cooker over medium-high heat. Add the onion and garlic and sauté 4 to 5 minutes, or until soft. Stir frequently so that the onion does not brown. Add the split peas and water.

Position the lid and lock in place. Raise the heat to high and bring to high pressure. Adjust the heat to stabilize the pressure and cook 10 minutes. Remove from the heat and lower the pressure using the cold-water-release method. Open the pressure cooker and stir well. The split-pea mixture should be very soft and thick. If still soupy, bring to a boil, lower the heat, and let simmer, stirring frequently, so that it does not stick and burn. Simmer until thick. Spoon into a mixing bowl and season with salt and pepper to taste. Let cool to room temperature.

When cool, beat the split peas with a kitchen spoon to a puree. Stir in the lemon juice and gradually add 2 tablespoons of olive oil. Spoon into a small serving bowl. Drizzle the remaining tablespoon of olive oil over the top and sprinkle with the capers. Serve at room temperature with pita-bread triangles.

6 SERVINGS

APPROXIMATE NUTRITIONAL ANALYSIS PER SERVING
247 calories, 7g protein, 20g carbohydrates, 16g fat, 0mg cholesterol, 765mg sodium

VEGETABLES

The following cooking times are provided as guidelines to be used in steaming vegetables in the pressure cooker. Cooking times can vary, depending on the quality and the individual piece sizes; maximum and minimum cooking times are given in some instances. When uncertain how long to cook something, always start with the shortest cooking time, since you can always continue cooking for an additional couple of minutes until the desired texture is reached.

Since water and liquids boil more slowly at altitudes of more than 2,000 feet above sea level, the cooking time and the amount of cooking liquid needed must be increased accordingly. Please refer to page 28 for additional information.

All cooking times listed begin once high or maximum pressure is reached.

APPROXIMATE COOKING TIMES

FRESH VEGETABLES	COOKING TIME	AMOUNT WATER
(Steamed on steamer basket or rack)		
Artichokes, medium whole, trimmed	6 to 8 minutes	1 cup
Artichokes, large whole, trimmed	9 to 11 minutes	1 cup
Artichoke, hearts	2 to 3 minutes	½ cup
Asparagus, thick whole	1 to 2 minutes	½ cup
Asparagus, thin whole	1 to 1½ minutes	½ cup
Beans, fava, shelled	4 minutes	¾ cup
Beans, green or wax, whole or piece	2 to 3 minutes	½ cup
Beans, lima, shelled	2 minutes	½ cup
Beets, small whole	12 minutes	1½ cups
Beets, large whole	20 minutes	2 cups
Beets, ¼-inch slices	4 minutes	¾ cup
Broccoli, florets	2 minutes	½ cup
Broccoli, spears	3 minutes	½ cup
Brussels sprouts, whole	4 minutes	¾ cup
Cabbage, red or green, ¼-inch shreds	1 minute	½ cup
Cabbage, red or green, quartered	3 to 4 minutes	¾ cup
Carrots, whole	6 to 8 minutes	1 cup
Carrots, 1-inch chunks	4 minutes	¾ cup
Carrots, ¼-inch slices	1 minute	½ cup
Cauliflower, florets	2 to 3 minutes	½ cup
Collard greens, coarsely chopped	5 minutes	1 cup
Corn, kernels	1 minute	½ cup
Corn on the cob	3 minutes	½ cup
Eggplant, sliced ⅛- to ¼-inch slices	2 to 3 minutes	½ cup
Eggplant, ½-inch chunks	3 minutes	½ cup
Escarole, coarsely chopped	1 to 2 minutes	½ cup
Kale, coarsely chopped	1 to 2 minutes	½ cup

FRESH VEGETABLES, CONTINUED	COOKING TIME	AMOUNT WATER
Okra, small pods	2 to 3 minutes	½ cup
Onions, whole, 1½-inch diameter	2 minutes	½ cup
Parsnips, 1-inch chunks	3 minutes	½ cup
Parsnips, ¼-inch slices	1 minute	½ cup
Peas, shelled	1 minute	½ cup
Potatoes, 1½-inch chunks	6 minutes	1 cup
Potatoes, new, small whole	5 minutes	1 cup
Pumpkin, 2-inch chunks	3 to 4 minutes	¾ cup
Rutabaga, 1-inch chunks	4 minutes	¾ cup
Spinach, fresh, coarsely chopped	2 minutes	½ cup
Spinach, fresh, whole leaves	3 minutes	½ cup
Squash, acorn, halved	7 minutes	1 cup
Squash, butternut, 1-inch chunks	4 minutes	¾ cup
Squash, pattypan, 2 pounds whole	11 minutes	1½ cups
Squash, spaghetti, 2 pounds whole	10 minutes	1½ cups
Squash, summer, zucchini or yellow, ½-inch slices	2 minutes	½ cup
Sweet potato, 1½-inch chunks	5 minutes	1 cup
Swiss chard, coarsely chopped	2 minutes	½ cup
Tomatoes, quartered	2 minutes	½ cup
Turnips, small, quartered	3 minutes	½ cup
Turnips, 1½-inch chunks	3 minutes	½ cup

APPROXIMATE COOKING TIMES

FROZEN VEGETABLES	COOKING TIME	AMOUNT WATER
(Steamed in steamer basket or rack)		
Asparagus	2 minutes	½ cup
Beans, green, wax, or french-cut	1 minute	½ cup
Beans, lima	2 minutes	½ cup
Broccoli, chopped, florets, or spears	2 minutes	½ cup
Brussels sprouts	2 minutes	½ cup
Cauliflower, florets	1 minute	½ cup
Corn, kernels	1 minute	½ cup
Corn on the cob	2 minutes	½ cup
Mixed vegetables	2 minutes	½ cup
Peas	1 minute	½ cup
Peas and carrots	1 minute	½ cup
Spinach	1 minute	½ cup
Squash, cut into 1-inch chunks	7 minutes	1 cup

BRAISED ARTICHOKES

ITALY, SPAIN, AND GREECE

Artichokes are probably the most Mediterranean of vegetables. They are grown throughout the region and enjoyed in many different guises. Rich in vitamin C and high in fiber, artichokes have been held in high esteem since the days of the ancient Romans, where according to the noted Roman scholar and writer Pliny, it was the most expensive of garden vegetables.

A single artichoke is actually an unopened flower bud from a thistle-like plant. Since the outer leaves of the bud are tough and inedible, they are torn off and discarded, revealing the delicate inner leaves. The tenderest part of the artichoke—the immature, pale, light-green center or heart—is eaten whole after the fuzzy core, or "choke," is removed.

The following recipe is a popular method for preparing the smaller buds or artichokes that grow on the side branches of the plant. These simple-to-prepare artichoke hearts can be served as part of an antipasto or as part of a collection of Spanish tapas or Greek *mezethes*.

Juice of 2 lemons
3 pounds very small baby
   artichokes
1/4 cup extra-virgin olive oil
3 cloves garlic, peeled and crushed
1 bay leaf
1 1/2 teaspoons salt

1/2 teaspoon whole black
   peppercorns
3/4 cup water
3 tablespoons sherry or
   white-wine vinegar
2 tablespoons minced parsley

Pour the lemon juice into a large bowl half-filled with water. Remove the stems from the artichokes with a sharp knife. Tear off and remove the tough outer leaves just until the center or light-green heart of the artichoke is exposed. Trim the base and cut off 1/4 to 1/2 inch from the top of the artichoke heart. Cut the artichokes in half and place in the water and lemon juice so that they do not discolor. After preparing all the artichokes, drain and place them in the pressure cooker with the olive oil, garlic, bay leaf, salt, peppercorns, and water.

Position the lid and lock in place. Place over high heat and bring to high pressure. Adjust the heat to stabilize the pressure and cook 2 minutes. Remove from heat and lower pressure using the cold-water-release method. Open the pressure cooker.

Remove the artichokes with a slotted spoon and place in a shallow serving dish. Cover and set aside.

Bring the cooking liquid to a boil and reduce until most of the water has evaporated. Remove from the heat. Add the vinegar and pour through a fine-mesh strainer over the cooked artichokes. Discard the garlic, bay leaf, and peppercorns. Let cool to room temperature. Sprinkle with parsley before serving.

4 SERVINGS

APPROXIMATE NUTRITIONAL ANALYSIS PER SERVING

199 calories, 5g protein, 19g carbohydrates, 14g fat, 0mg cholesterol, 924mg sodium

Marinated Squid and Fennel Salad (page 136)

Stuffed Vegetables (page 124)

Mussels à la Cataplana (page 131)

Vegetable Soup with Basil (page 56) and Chicken Soup with Lemon and Mint (page 50).

Risotto with Spring Vegetables (page 85)

Venetian-Style Artichokes (page 97)

Asparagus Frittata (page 100)

Stuffed Pork Bundles (page 163)

Chickpeas with Spinach (page 78)

Warm Shrimp and Bean Salad (page 66)

STUFFED ARTICHOKES
Carciofi Ripieni

While small baby artichokes can be eaten whole, larger artichokes, which grow from the center stem of the plant, are definitely a finger food. After the tough outer leaves are removed and the vegetable is trimmed, it is usually braised or steamed. To eat an artichoke, pull the cooked leaves off one at a time and scrape the inner side of the leaf through your teeth to remove the soft flesh. As you continue to remove the outer leaves you will eventually reach the tender, pale-green center, or heart, which can be eaten whole after the choke is removed.

One of my favorite ways of preparing large artichokes is to stuff them with a savory filling, as is done in many regions of Italy. The many advantages to cooking artichokes in a pressure cooker include the amount of time saved. For this recipe the small amount of liquid used in cooking means the stuffing does not become as wet as when using traditional cooking methods. Two popular variations follow.

VENETIAN-STYLE ARTICHOKES

♦ *Carciofi alla Venezia, Italy*

4 large artichokes (approximately 8 to 10 ounces each), untrimmed
10 tablespoons plain, dry bread crumbs
2 cloves garlic, peeled and minced
1 tablespoon minced parsley
2 tablespoons freshly grated Parmesan cheese

Large pinch freshly ground black pepper
6 tablespoons extra-virgin olive oil
1 cup water
1 teaspoon salt

Remove the stems from the artichokes with a sharp knife. Tear off and discard the top two to three layers of tough outer leaves. Trim the base so that the artichokes stand flat. Cut off $1/2$ to 1 inch from the tops of the artichokes. Carefully open the center of the artichoke to expose the center leaves and choke. Pull out and remove any thorny leaves, which are usually tinged with purple. With a teaspoon, scoop out and discard any fuzzy matter from the center choke. Set aside.

Prepare the filling by mixing together the bread crumbs, garlic, parsley, Parmesan, black pepper, and 4 tablespoons of the olive oil in a small bowl. Starting with the outer leaves, stuff a small amount of the filling between the leaves, taking care not to break off the leaves. Sprinkle the tops with any remaining filling.

Pour the water into the pressure cooker. Add the salt and stir to mix. Place the prepared artichokes in the pressure cooker standing up. Drizzle the remaining 2 tablespoons of olive oil over the artichokes.

Position the lid and lock in place. Place over high heat and bring to high pressure. Adjust the heat to stabilize the pressure and cook 7 minutes. Remove from the heat and lower the pressure using the cold-water-release method. Open the pressure cooker. Carefully remove the artichokes using a slotted spoon and place in individual serving bowls. Spoon a couple of tablespoons of the cooking liquid over each artichoke before serving.

4 SERVINGS

APPROXIMATE NUTRITIONAL ANALYSIS PER SERVING

392 calories, 7g protein, 43g carbohydrates, 22g fat, 3mg cholesterol, 730mg sodium

HOME-STYLE STUFFED ARTICHOKES

◆ *Carciofi Ripieni alla Cassalinga, Italy*

4 large artichokes (approximately 8 to 10 ounces each), untrimmed	1 tablespoon minced parsley
2 large eggs	Pinch freshly ground black pepper
1/4 cup freshly grated Pecorino Romano cheese	1 cup water
	1 teaspoon salt
1 clove garlic, peeled and minced	1 bay leaf
	2 tablespoons extra-virgin olive oil

Remove the stems from the artichokes with a sharp knife. Tear off and discard the top two or three layers of tough outer leaves. Trim the base so that the artichokes stand flat. Cut off 1/2 to 1 inch from the tops of the artichokes. Carefully open the center of the artichoke to expose the center leaves and choke. Pull out and remove any thorny leaves, which are usually tinged with purple. With a teaspoon, scoop out and discard any fuzzy matter from the center choke. Set aside.

Prepare the filling by beating together the eggs, Romano, garlic, parsley, and black pepper.

Pour the water into the pressure cooker. Add the salt and stir to mix. Add the bay leaf. Carefully open up the artichoke leaves slightly, starting from the center and working outward, taking care not to break off the leaves. Place the prepared artichokes in the pressure cooker standing up. Drizzle an equal amount of the egg mixture over the artichokes, being certain to spoon some into the center. Drizzle with the olive oil.

Position the lid and lock in place. Place over high heat and bring to high pressure. Adjust the heat to stabilize the pressure and cook 7 minutes. Remove from heat and lower pressure using the cold-water-release method. Open the pressure cooker. Carefully remove the artichokes using a slotted spoon and place in individual serving bowls. Spoon a couple of tablespoons of the cooking liquid over each artichoke before serving.

4 SERVINGS

APPROXIMATE NUTRITIONAL ANALYSIS PER SERVING

263 calories, 9g protein, 31g carbohydrates, 3g fat, 12mg cholesterol, 648mg sodium

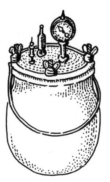

ASPARAGUS FRITTATA
Frittata di Asparagi

Frittate, the oversized Italian version of omelets, are enjoyed throughout Italy as a light lunch or supper. Usually made with whatever is available in the refrigerator, they are made with a wide variety of vegetables and even leftover unsauced pasta. Frittate can either be prepared on the stove in a skillet or baked in the oven, as with this asparagus frittata.

$3/4$ cup water
1 pound asparagus, trimmed
Olive oil for greasing
$1/2$ cup ricotta
8 large eggs, lightly beaten
2 tablespoons water

$1/4$ cup freshly grated Parmesan
  cheese
1 tablespoon minced parsley
$1/2$ teaspoon salt
$1/8$ teaspoon freshly ground black
  pepper

Pour the water into the pressure cooker. Place the asparagus in the pressure cooker steamer basket and place on the trivet in the pressure cooker.

Position the lid and lock in place. Place over high heat and bring to high pressure. Adjust heat to stabilize pressure and cook $1^{1}/_{2}$ to $2^{1}/_{2}$ minutes, depending on the thickness of the asparagus (consult the cooking time information, page 92). Remove from the heat and lower the pressure using the cold-water-release method. Open the pressure cooker. Carefully remove the steamer basket. Let cool to room temperature.

Preheat oven to 375°F. Grease a 10 x 8-inch baking dish with olive oil. Layer the asparagus in rows on the bottom of the dish. Spread the ricotta over the asparagus. In a mixing bowl, beat together the eggs, water, Parmesan, parsley, salt, and black pepper. Pour the egg mixture over the asparagus. Bake for 20 to 25 minutes, or until the egg is set. Remove from the oven. Let cool 5 minutes before serving.

6 SERVINGS

APPROXIMATE NUTRITIONAL ANALYSIS PER SERVING
164 calories, 14g protein, 5g carbohydrates, 10g fat, 293mg cholesterol, 373mg sodium

BROCCOLI DI RAPE AND SAUSAGES
Broccoli di Rape e Salsicce

Broccoli di rape, a pleasantly bitter, leafy green with scattered clusters of broccoli-like buds, is extremely popular in the Italian region of Apulia, on Italy's Adriatic coast. There, it is braised quickly in a bit of olive oil and garlic, then served with fennel-flavored Italian sausage over pasta.

When purchasing broccoli di rape, which is available at most supermarkets and greengrocers, be certain that the buds are firm and closed, to assure that the broccoli di rape has not passed its prime.

6 tablespoons olive oil
4 links sweet Italian sausage
  with fennel
1/2 cup water
4 cloves garlic, peeled and
  crushed
2 pounds broccoli di rape,
  trimmed of all thick
  stems
1/4 teaspoon crushed red
  pepper

1 teaspoon salt
1 cup Rich Chicken Stock (page
  47) or canned chicken
  broth
1 pound orecchietti or penne rigati
  pasta, cooked *al dente*
Freshly grated Pecorino Romano
  cheese for serving

Heat 2 tablespoons of the olive oil in the pressure cooker over high heat. Add the sausages. Cook over medium-high heat until just browned. Add the water.

Position the lid and lock in place. Raise the heat to high and bring to high pressure. Adjust the heat to stabilize the pressure and cook 5 minutes. Remove from the heat and lower the pressure using the cold-water-release method. Open the pressure cooker. Remove the sausages. Pour out and discard the cooking liquid.

Add the remaining 4 tablespoons of olive oil to the pressure cooker. Add the garlic and sauté over medium-high heat until golden. Add the broccoli di rape, crushed red pepper, salt, stock, and cooked sausages. Mix well. Position the lid on the pressure cooker and lock in place. Raise the heat to high and bring to high pressure. Adjust the heat to stabilize the pressure and cook 1 1/2 minutes. Remove from the heat and lower the pressure using the cold-water-release method. Open the pressure cooker. Taste and adjust for salt.

In a large serving bowl, mix the pasta with the broccoli di rape and sausages. Serve with the cheese.

4 SERVINGS

APPROXIMATE NUTRITIONAL ANALYSIS PER SERVING

864 calories, 36g protein, 88g carbohydrates, 42g fat, 55mg cholesterol, 1604mg sodium

CARROT SALAD

MOROCCO

This wonderfully refreshing carrot salad combines the culinary elements of the Mediterranean with exotic spices of the East, which were brought to the region hundreds of years ago by Arabic traders. Serve as a side dish or as part of a collection of small plates of varied appetizers.

3/4 cup water

1 pound large carrots, peeled and
  cut diagonally in pieces 1/4 inch
  thick and 1 1/2 inches long

1/4 cup extra-virgin olive oil

2 tablespoons freshly squeezed
  lemon juice

1 clove garlic, peeled and minced

1 1/2 teaspoons sugar

1 teaspoon paprika

1/2 teaspoon salt

1/2 teaspoon ground cumin

1/8 teaspoon ground cinnamon

1 pinch cayenne pepper

1 tablespoon minced parsley

Pour the water into the pressure cooker. Place the carrots in the steamer basket and place on the trivet in the pressure cooker.

Position the lid and lock in place. Place over high heat and bring to high pressure. Adjust the heat to stabilize the pressure and cook 30 seconds to parboil the carrots. Remove from the heat and lower the pressure using the cold-water-release method. Open the pressure cooker and carefully remove the steamer basket. Place the carrots in a serving bowl.

Prepare the vinaigrette by whisking together the olive oil, lemon juice, garlic, and spices. Pour the vinaigrette over the warm carrots and toss well. Let sit until carrots are cooled to room temperature, tossing periodically. Sprinkle with the minced parsley before serving.

4 SERVINGS

APPROXIMATE NUTRITIONAL ANALYSIS PER SERVING

181 calories, 1g protein, 15g carbohydrates, 14g fat, 0mg cholesterol, 308mg sodium

CAULIFLOWER SALAD
Insalata di Cavolfiore

Cauliflower, one of the most popular vegetables in Italy, was introduced to the Italians by the Moors during their period of expansion in the Middle Ages. Enjoyed in many different ways, cauliflower is commonly prepared in Italy as a salad dressed in olive oil and vinegar with anchovies, garlic, and black olives.

1 medium-sized head cauliflower	1 clove garlic, peeled
³/₄ cup water	¹/₂ teaspoon salt
¹/₄ cup extra-virgin olive oil	¹/₂ cup brine-cured, Italian black
2 tablespoons white-wine vinegar	olives
1 tablespoon capers, rinsed	1 tablespoon minced parsley
2 anchovies	

Cut and remove the hard stalks from the cauliflower. Break or cut into small florets.

Pour the water into the pressure cooker. Place the cauliflower in the steamer basket and place on the trivet in the pressure cooker.

Position the lid and lock in place. Place over high heat and bring to high pressure. Adjust the heat to stabilize the pressure and cook 2 minutes. Remove from the heat and lower the pressure using the cold-water-release method. Open the pressure cooker. Carefully remove the steamer basket. Rinse the cauliflower at once under cold water to stop the cooking process. Drain well and set aside in a large serving bowl.

Prepare the vinaigrette: Place the olive oil, vinegar, capers, anchovies, garlic, and salt in a blender jar and blend until smooth. Taste and adjust for salt. Pour the vinaigrette over the cauliflower and toss gently. Garnish with the black olives and sprinkle with parsley.

4 SERVINGS

APPROXIMATE NUTRITIONAL ANALYSIS PER SERVING

158 calories, 2g protein, 4g carbohydrates, 16g fat, 2mg cholesterol, 651mg sodium

EGGPLANT SPREAD
Baba Ghanouj

A native of India, eggplant was introduced into the cuisine of the Mediterranean region by Arabic traders during the twelfth century. It was originally thought to cause madness, leprosy, and a variety of other maladies, and not until the late eighteenth century was eggplant finally accepted as safe to eat.

Baba ghanouj is a delicious, Middle Eastern eggplant spread. The eggplant is traditionally roasted and charred over a wood fire or in an oven. Nevertheless, I discovered that by steaming the eggplant in a pressure cooker and then blending it with browned garlic I could achieve a similar, smoky flavor in a fraction of the time. The results are sublime.

1 large eggplant, about 1½ pounds, peeled and cut into ½-inch dice	3 large cloves garlic, peeled and minced
Salt	2 tablespoons freshly squeezed lemon juice
¾ cup water	2 tablespoons minced parsley
2 tablespoons extra-virgin olive oil	

Put the diced eggplant in a large colander. Sprinkle lightly with salt and toss. Let sit one hour to drain. Apply pressure on the eggplant to remove any excess liquid.

Pour the water into the pressure cooker. Place the eggplant in the steamer basket and place on trivet. Position the lid and lock in place. Place over high heat and bring to high pressure. Adjust the heat to stabilize the pressure and cook 3 minutes. Remove from the heat and lower the pressure using the cold-water-release method. Open the pressure cooker and carefully remove the steamer basket. The cooked eggplant should be very soft. If not, reposition the lid on the pressure cooker and cook an additional 1 to 2 minutes under high pressure.

Place the steamed eggplant in the bowl of a food processor and pulse just until smooth. Do not overprocess.

Heat the olive oil and garlic in a small saucepan over medium-high heat. Remove from the heat once the garlic begins to sizzle. Immediately add the sautéed garlic and oil along with the lemon juice and parsley to the pureed eggplant in the food processor. Blend the mixture together by holding down the pulse button for 15 seconds. Taste and adjust for salt. Serve with pita bread or Arabic flat bread.

6 SERVINGS

APPROXIMATE NUTRITIONAL ANALYSIS PER SERVING

130 calories, 74g protein, 8g carbohydrates, 5g fat, 0mg cholesterol, 360mg sodium

SWEET-AND-SOUR SICILIAN EGGPLANT
Caponata

ITALY

Variously subjected to Greek, Roman, Moorish, Norman, French, and Spanish rule, Sicily has a cuisine that clearly reflects the influence of each of these powers. One of the most significant, however, was that of the Moors, who ruled Sicily for a period of three hundred years. During that time they introduced to the Sicilians advanced agricultural methods, new fruits and vegetables from the Orient, and the use of sugar in place of honey. In fact, a clear indication of Moorish influence in Mediterranean cooking is the combination of sweet and savory, as in this traditional Sicilian eggplant dish that can be served as an appetizer or a side dish.

2 pounds medium-sized
   eggplants, peeled and cut into
   1/2-inch dice
Salt
1/4 cup olive oil
1 large onion, coarsely chopped
1 cup canned tomato puree
2 stalks celery, cut into 1/4-inch dice

4 tablespoons capers, drained and
   rinsed under water
3 tablespoons sugar
1 teaspoon salt
1/8 teaspoon freshly ground black
   pepper
1/2 cup white-wine vinegar

Put the diced eggplant in a large colander, sprinkle lightly with the salt, and toss. Let sit 1 hour to drain. Press on the eggplant to remove any excess liquid.

Heat 2 tablespoons of the olive oil in the pressure cooker over high heat. Add the eggplant and sauté stirring frequently, 4 to 5 minutes, until the eggplant just begins to take on some color. Remove the sauteéd eggplant to a large bowl with a slotted spoon. Add the remaining olive oil to the pressure cooker. Add the onion and sauté over medium-high heat 4 to 5 minutes, or until soft, stirring frequently so that the onion does not brown. Add the tomato puree.

Position the lid and lock in place. Raise the heat to high and bring to high pressure. Adjust the heat to stabilize the pressure and cook 2 minutes. Remove from the heat and lower the pressure using the cold-water-release method. Open the pressure cooker, add the eggplant and the remaining ingredients, and stir to blend. Position the lid on the pressure cooker and lock in place. Place over high heat and bring to high pressure. Adjust the heat to stabilize the pressure. Cook 3 minutes. Remove from the heat and lower the pressure using the cold-water-release method. Open the pressure cooker and carefully spoon the caponata into a large serving bowl. Let cool to room temperature before serving.

8 SERVINGS

APPROXIMATE NUTRITIONAL ANALYSIS PER SERVING

132 calories, 2g protein, 17g carbohydrates, 7g fat, 0mg cholesterol, 705mg sodium

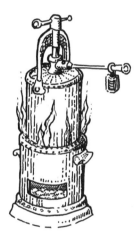

QUICK PICKLED EGGPLANT
Melanzane sott'Olio

I have enjoyed the following recipe many times at the home of Argentinean friends. Since Argentina was settled by mostly Italian and Spanish immigrants, the origin of this dish is undoubtedly Mediterranean.

By steaming the eggplant before mixing it with the vinaigrette, you are able to enjoy eating it almost immediately without having to wait for the pickling mixture to penetrate the raw eggplant over a period of time, as you would when following traditional methods.

1 1/2 pounds long, thin Italian or Japanese eggplant, peeled and sliced 1/8 inch thick
Salt
3/4 cup water
1/4 cup olive oil
2 tablespoons white-wine vinegar

1 clove garlic, peeled and minced
1/2 teaspoon oregano
1/2 teaspoon salt
1/8 teaspoon freshly ground black pepper
1 sprig mint, torn into pieces (optional)

Put the eggplant slices in a large colander, sprinkling lightly with salt. Let sit 1 hour to drain. Press on the eggplant to remove any excess liquid.

Pour the water into the pressure cooker. Layer the eggplant in the steamer basket and place on the trivet. Position the lid and lock in place. Place over high heat and bring to high pressure. Adjust the heat to stabilize the pressure and cook 2 minutes. Remove from the heat and lower the pressure using the cold-water-release method. Open the pressure cooker and carefully remove the steamer basket.

Prepare the vinaigrette by whisking together the olive oil, vinegar, garlic, oregano, salt, and black pepper. Place a layer of eggplant on a shallow serving dish. Drizzle with some of the vinaigrette and, if desired, sprinkle with some mint. Cover with another layer of eggplant, vinaigrette, and mint until you have used all the eggplant, ending with a final drizzling of vinaigrette. Cover with plastic wrap or foil and let sit at least four hours to allow the flavors to blend.

6 SERVINGS

APPROXIMATE NUTRITIONAL ANALYSIS PER SERVING
89 calories, 0g protein, 1g carbohydrates, 9g fat, 0mg cholesterol, 356mg sodium

FAVA BEANS WITH CURED HAM
Favas Ribatejana

- *Habas con Jamón, Spain*
- *Fave al Prosciutto, Italy*

Fava beans are a staple of the Mediterranean region. Appearing in spring, they are often eaten sautéed with onions and cured ham as a first course, as in this popular recipe.

When buying fava beans look for bright-green, firm, fat pods that are not too thick, otherwise the fava beans inside will be tough. If they are very fresh, you can also cut the pods into long, thin strips and cook them along with the beans.

¼ cup olive oil	3 pounds fava beans, shelled
1 large onion, chopped	½ teaspoon salt
1 clove garlic, peeled and minced	⅛ teaspoon freshly ground black
4-ounce slice Italian prosciutto,	pepper
Portuguese *presunto*, or Spanish	¾ cup water
jamón serrano, cut into ¼-inch	¼ cup minced parsley
dice	

Heat the olive oil in the pressure cooker over medium-high heat. Add the onion, garlic, and ham. Sauté 4 to 5 minutes, or until the onion is soft. Stir frequently so that the onion does not brown. Add the fava beans, salt, black pepper, and water.

Position the lid and lock in place. Raise the heat to high and bring to high pressure. Adjust the heat to stabilize the pressure and cook 7 minutes. Remove from the heat and lower the pressure using the cold-water-release method. Open the pressure cooker, taste, and adjust for salt and pepper. Stir in the parsley before serving.

4 SERVINGS

APPROXIMATE NUTRITIONAL ANALYSIS PER SERVING

353 calories, 20g protein, 35g carbohydrates, 16g fat, 13mg cholesterol, 1829mg sodium

SAUTÉED MUSHROOMS
Funghi Trippati

The literal translation of this recipe's name from Italian is "tripe-style" mushrooms, and the mushrooms are prepared in a sauce similarly used in Italy to cook tripe, usually beef stomach lining. These sautéed mushrooms are delicious and make a perfect side dish.

1/4 cup olive oil	3 tablespoons tomato paste
2 cloves garlic, peeled and crushed	5 tablespoons water
20 ounces white mushrooms,	1 teaspoon dried oregano
stems trimmed, wiped clean,	1 teaspoon salt
and cut into 1/4-inch-thick slices	1/8 teaspoon black pepper

Heat the olive oil in the pressure cooker over high heat. Add the garlic and sauté 1 minute. Add the mushrooms and sauté 2 minutes, stirring constantly. Stir in the tomato paste, water, oregano, salt, and black pepper.

Position the lid and lock in place. Raise the heat to high and bring to high pressure. Adjust the heat to stabilize the pressure and cook 2 minutes. Remove from the heat and lower the pressure using the cold-water-release method. Open the pressure cooker, taste, and adjust for salt and pepper.

4 SERVINGS

APPROXIMATE NUTRITIONAL ANALYSIS PER SERVING

161 calories, 3g protein, 8g carbohydrates, 14g fat, 0mg cholesterol, 633mg sodium

ROMAN-STYLE PRESSURE-ROASTED POTATOES
Patate Arroste alla Romana

Potatoes roasted in the same pan as a leg of lamb or a breast of veal are commonplace in the simple yet delicious country-style cooking of Rome. While the potatoes may not be as crisp when made in a pressure cooker, they are equally tasty and great for when you are short on time. For best results, be sure to brown the potatoes evenly, on all sides, over high heat. I find that Idaho or russet potatoes give the best results.

1/4 cup olive oil
2 pounds Idaho or russet potatoes, peeled and cut into 2-inch pieces, rinsed under cold water and patted dry
1 large onion, cut in half and thinly sliced

1 1/2 teaspoons salt
1/4 teaspoon freshly ground black pepper
1 teaspoon dried rosemary leaves (optional)
1/2 cup water

Heat the olive oil in the pressure cooker over high heat. Cook the potatoes in two batches so as not to overcrowd, and brown evenly on all sides, approximately 6 to 8 minutes. Remove to a bowl with a slotted spoon when browned. Add the onion and sauté 4 to 5 minutes, or until the onion just begins to brown. Stir frequently so that the onion does not burn. Add the browned potatoes and the remaining ingredients and stir to mix.

Position the lid and lock in place. Raise the heat to high and bring to high pressure. Adjust the heat to stabilize the pressure and cook 5 minutes. Remove from the heat and let the pressure drop naturally. Open pressure cooker, taste, and adjust for salt and pepper.

8 SERVINGS

APPROXIMATE NUTRITIONAL ANALYSIS PER SERVING

228 calories, 5g protein, 39g carbohydrates, 7g fat, 0mg cholesterol, 413mg sodium

POTATO AND RED-PEPPER SPREAD
Ajilimojili

This unusual recipe is from Jaen, a province in Andalucía in the the south of Spain. Potatoes and peppers were first introduced into the Mediterranean diet from the Americas in the early sixteenth century. *Ajilimojili* is delicious served as an appetizer spread on thin slices of toasted, crusty bread or as a side dish with grilled fish, meat, or poultry.

1 cup water
1 pound boiling potatoes, peeled
  and cut into 1-inch pieces
1 pound red peppers, cut in half,
  cored, and seeded
2 tablespoons extra-virgin olive oil

1½ tablespoons sherry or
  white-wine vinegar
1 teaspoon salt
⅛ teaspoon freshly ground black
  pepper

Pour the water into the pressure cooker. Place the steamer basket on the trivet. Fill with the potatoes and then the red pepper.

Position the lid and lock in place. Place over high heat and bring to high pressure. Adjust the heat to stabilize the pressure and cook 7 minutes. Remove from the heat and lower the pressure using the cold-water-release method. Open the pressure cooker. Carefully remove the steamer basket.

Remove the peppers and carefully peel or scrape off as much of the skin as possible. Place the peppers and potatoes in a large mixing bowl. Add the remaining ingredients and mash with a potato masher or a large fork. Do not overmash. The mixture should be chunky yet well blended. Taste and adjust for salt and pepper.

4 SERVINGS

APPROXIMATE NUTRITIONAL ANALYSIS PER SERVING

171 calories, 3g protein, 26g carbohydrates, 7g fat, 0mg cholesterol, 539mg sodium

RUSSIAN SALAD
Ensaladilla Rusa

♦ *Insalata Russa, Italy*

Try as hard as I may, I am still unable to discover the origin of the name of this dish and therefore can only surmise that the basic recipe was brought to southern Europe by members of the royal court who were related by marriage to the rulers of Poland during the sixteenth century—thus the Russian name.

This is a delicious, albeit very filling, salad that is typically prepared at home as a cold lunch or supper in the summer or enjoyed at tapas bars in Spain with bread or *picos*, little bread sticks. Since there are slight differences between the Spanish and Italian versions of this salad, I have provided a basic recipe along with the different variations for each. The choice is yours.

Basic Recipe:

1 cup water

2 pounds boiling potatoes, peeled and cut into 1/2-inch dice

2 small carrots, peeled and cut into 1/4-inch dice

1 1/4 cups mayonnaise

2 tablespoons white-wine vinegar

1/2 teaspoon salt

Ensaladilla Rusa:

1 (4-ounce) jar roasted peppers, drained and patted dry

1/2 cup small green Spanish olives stuffed with pimientos, drained

1/2 cup green peas, fresh or frozen, cooked until tender

1 (3-ounce) can tuna fish, packed in oil, drained

1 cup shredded romaine lettuce

Insalata Russa:

2 small beets, peeled, cut into 1/4-inch dice

1/4 pound string beans, trimmed and cut into 1/2-inch pieces

2 tablespoons chopped tart gherkins

1 tablespoon small capers for garnish, rinsed under water and patted dry

Pour the water into the pressure cooker. If preparing Ensaladilla Rusa, place the potatoes and carrots in the steamer basket on the trivet in the pressure cooker. Cut half of 1 roasted pepper in strips and reserve for garnish. Coarsely chop remaining peppers. Slice 3 olives for garnish and reserve remainder. When preparing Insalata Russa, first place the diced beets, then the potatoes, carrots, and string beans in the steamer basket.

Position the lid and lock in place. Place over high heat and bring to high pressure. Adjust the heat to stabilize the pressure, and cook 6 minutes. Remove from the heat and lower the pressure using the cold-water-release method. Open the pressure cooker. If the vegetables are not yet tender, reposition the lid on the pressure cooker and cook under high pressure an additional 1 to 2 minutes.

Open the pressure cooker and carefully remove the steamer basket. Place the cooked vegetables in a large mixing bowl and let cool until just warm. In a small bowl mix together ³⁄₄ cup of the mayonnaise with the vinegar.

To prepare Ensaladilla Rusa, add the peas, tuna fish, shredded lettuce, green olives, and chopped roasted peppers to the vegetables. Toss to mix. Add the mayonnaise dressing and toss. Taste and adjust for salt. Spoon the potato salad on a serving plate, mounding slightly. Smooth the top with a spatula and evenly spread with the remaining ¹⁄₂ cup of mayonnaise. Decoratively place the sliced roasted peppers and olives on top.

To prepare Insalata Russa, add the chopped pickles to the vegetables. Toss to mix. Add the mayonnaise dressing and toss to blend. Taste and adjust for salt. Spoon the potato salad on a serving plate, mounding slightly. Smooth the top with a spatula and evenly spread with the remaining ¹⁄₂ cup of mayonnaise. Sprinkle with the capers.

8 SERVINGS

APPROXIMATE NUTRITIONAL ANALYSIS PER SERVING OF ENSALADILLA RUSA

383 calories, 6g protein, 26g carbohydrates, 30g fat, 22mg cholesterol, 598mg sodium

APPROXIMATE NUTRITIONAL ANALYSIS PER SERVING OF INSALATA RUSSA

355 calories, 3g protein, 26g carbohydrates, 28g fat, 20mg cholesterol, 393mg sodium

POTATO PIE
Torta di Patate

My grandmother has been preparing this recipe for holiday meals and special dinners for as long as I can remember. Originating in the Sorrento area of Naples, *torta di patate* is a perfect accompaniment to roasted meats or poultry.

1 cup water

2½ pounds boiling potatoes (about 8 medium-sized), peeled and cut into 1½-inch pieces

2 large eggs

⅓ cup freshly grated Pecorino Romano cheese

⅛ teaspoon freshly ground black pepper

⅓ cup plain, dry bread crumbs

4 ounces provolone cheese, cut into ⅛-inch dice

4 ounces mozzarella cheese, cut into ⅛-inch dice

2 ounces hard Italian salami or dried sausage, cut into ⅛-inch dice

1½ tablespoons solid vegetable shortening

Pour the water into the pressure cooker. Place the potatoes in the steamer basket and place on the trivet. Position the lid and lock in place. Place over high heat and bring to high pressure. Adjust the heat to stabilize the pressure and cook 7 minutes. Remove from the heat and lower the pressure using the cold-water-release method. Open the pressure cooker. If the potatoes are not yet fork-tender, reposition the lid on the pressure cooker and continue cooking under high pressure an additional 2 to 3 minutes. Remove from heat and lower the pressure using the cold-water-release method. Open the pressure cooker and carefully remove the steamer basket.

Process the hot potatoes through a ricer or food mill into a large mixing bowl. Let cool to room temperature.

In a mixing bowl, lightly beat the eggs with the cheese and black pepper. Add to the potatoes, along with 2 tablespoons of the bread crumbs, the provolone and mozzarella cheeses, and salami. Stir just to blend. Do not overmix.

Preheat oven to 425°F.

Lightly grease a 10x8-inch baking dish with ½ tablespoon shortening. Sprinkle the sides and bottom of the dish with 2 tablespoons of the bread crumbs. Spoon the potato mixture into the prepared baking dish. Smooth with a spatula. Sprinkle the top with the remaining bread crumbs. Dot the top with the remaining shortening. Bake 20 to 25 minutes, or until the top is golden brown. Remove from the oven and let cool 10 minutes before serving.

8 SERVINGS

APPROXIMATE NUTRITIONAL ANALYSIS PER SERVING

299 calories, 14g protein, 28g carbohydrates, 15g fat, 84mg cholesterol, 455mg sodium

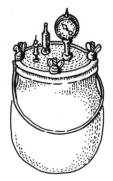

STRING BEANS AND POTATOES
Judias Verdes con Patatas

Simple, steamed string beans and potatoes drizzled with fruity, extra-virgin olive oil and seasoned with fresh minced garlic, salt, and black pepper, is simplicity at its best. Serve as a side dish or as the main course of a light supper with a *caprese* salad— vine-ripened tomatoes and fresh mozzarella cheese.

1 cup water
1 pound boiling potatoes, peeled
    and cut into 2-inch pieces
1½ pounds string beans, trimmed
    and cut in half

3 tablespoons extra-virgin olive oil
2 cloves garlic, peeled and minced
Salt to taste
Freshly ground black pepper to
    taste

Pour the water into the pressure cooker. Place the potatoes in the steamer basket and place on the trivet. Layer the string beans on top of the potatoes. Position the lid and lock in place. Place over high heat and bring to high pressure. Adjust the heat to stabilize the pressure and cook 6 minutes. Remove from the heat and lower the pressure using the cold-water-release method. Open the pressure cooker and carefully remove the steamer basket with the cooked string beans and potatoes.

In a large, shallow serving bowl or platter toss the string beans and potatoes with the olive oil, minced garlic, and salt and black pepper to taste.

4 SERVINGS

APPROXIMATE NUTRITIONAL ANALYSIS PER SERVING

228 calories, 5g protein, 32g carbohydrates, 11g fat, 0mg cholesterol, 142mg sodium

STRING BEAN SALAD WITH POTATOES
Insalata di Fagiolini con Patate

I usually serve this salad in the summer with barbecued meats or chicken that have been marinated in olive oil, lemon juice, and garlic.

1 cup water

1 pound boiling potatoes, peeled and cut into 1½-inch pieces

1 pound string beans, trimmed and cut in half

4 tablespoons extra-virgin olive oil

2 tablespoons red-wine vinegar

½ teaspoon dried oregano

1 teaspoon salt

⅛ teaspoon freshly ground black pepper

2 medium-sized, vine-ripened tomatoes, cut into wedges and seeded

1 small red onion, peeled, cut in half, and thinly sliced

8 basil leaves, torn in small pieces

Pour the water into the pressure cooker. Place the potatoes in the steamer basket on the trivet. Layer the string beans on top of the potatoes.

Position the lid and lock in place. Place over high heat and bring to high pressure. Adjust the heat to stabilize the pressure, and cook 6 minutes. Remove from the heat and lower the pressure using the cold-water-release method. Open the pressure cooker and carefully remove the steamer basket. Place the cooked string beans and potatoes in a large serving bowl and let cool to room temperature.

Prepare the vinaigrette by whisking together the olive oil, vinegar, oregano, salt, and black pepper. Pour the vinaigrette over the string beans and potatoes and toss.

Before serving, toss in the cut-up tomatoes, red onion, and basil. Taste and adjust for salt.

4 SERVINGS

APPROXIMATE NUTRITIONAL ANALYSIS PER SERVING

261 calories, 5g protein, 33g carbohydrates, 14g fat, 0mg cholesterol, 546mg sodium

TWICE-COOKED STRING BEANS
Fagiolini Riafatti

ITALY

RED-DRESSED GREEN BEANS

♦ *Haricots Verts en Robe Carlate, France*

"Twice cooked" in the name of this recipe refers to the initial steaming of the string beans in the pressure cooker and then a quick braising in a garlicky tomato sauce, to which the French recipe name so aptly refers. The addition of fresh basil infuses a definite Mediterranean flavor.

1 cup water	1 teaspoon salt
1½ pounds string beans, trimmed; left whole	⅛ teaspoon freshly ground black pepper
2 tablespoons olive oil	¼ cup water
2 cloves garlic, peeled and minced	6 basil leaves, torn into small
¾ cup canned, crushed tomatoes	pieces

Pour the water into the pressure cooker. Place the string beans in the steamer basket on the trivet. Position the lid and lock in place. Place over high heat and bring to high pressure. Adjust the heat to stabilize the pressure and cook 6 minutes. Remove from the heat and lower the pressure using the cold-water-release method. Open the pressure cooker and carefully remove the steamer basket.

Discard the cooking liquid. Rinse the pressure cooker and towel dry. Heat the olive oil in the pressure cooker over high heat. Add the garlic and sauté 1 minute. Add the tomatoes, salt, black pepper, and water. Position the lid and lock in place. Raise the heat to high and bring to high pressure. Adjust the heat to stabilize the pressure and cook 3 minutes. Remove from the heat and lower the pressure using the cold-water-release method. Open the pressure cooker. Add the cooked string beans and the basil. Toss to mix and warm over low heat until heated through. Taste and adjust for salt and pepper.

4 SERVINGS

APPROXIMATE NUTRITIONAL ANALYSIS PER SERVING

224 calories, 3g protein, 14g carbohydrates, 7g fat, 0mg cholesterol, 612mg sodium

MIXED VEGETABLE STEW
Menestra de Verduras

This mixed vegetable stew was created by frugal Spanish housewives as a way to turn leftovers into a one-pot meal, using whatever was on hand. Today *menestra* is usually made in late spring, taking advantage of the reappearance of tender garden vegetables.

3 tablespoons olive oil
1 large onion, chopped fine
2 cloves garlic, peeled and minced
4-ounce slice Italian prosciutto or Spanish *jamón serrano*, cut into ¼-inch dice
8 small, baby artichokes, stem and tough outer leaves removed until center or heart is visible, top ¼ inch trimmed, cut in half
2 medium red or white new potatoes, peeled and cut into ½-inch dice
2 large carrots, peeled and cut into ¼-inch dice

1 cup peas, fresh or frozen
1 pound fava beans, shelled
½ pound string beans, trimmed and cut in half
2 teaspoons flour
1 cup Rich Chicken Stock (page 47), Rich Vegetable Stock (page 46), or canned broth
2 tablespoons minced parsley
Salt to taste
Freshly ground black pepper to taste

Heat the olive oil in the pressure cooker over medium-high heat. Add the onion, garlic, and prosciutto and sauté 4 to 5 minutes, or until the onion is soft. Stir frequently so that the onion does not brown. Add the vegetables and cook 2 minutes, stirring constantly. Sprinkle the vegetable mixture with the flour, salt, and black pepper and stir to mix. Add the stock.

Position the lid and lock in place. Raise the heat to high and bring to high pressure. Adjust heat to stabilize pressure, and cook 4 minutes. Remove from heat and lower pressure using the cold-water-release method. Open the pressure cooker. Stir in the parsley. Taste and adjust for salt and pepper.

4 SERVINGS

APPROXIMATE NUTRITIONAL ANALYSIS PER SERVING
531 calories, 31g protein, 80g carbohydrates, 14g fat, 14mg cholesterol, 721mg sodium

VEGETABLE STEW WITH COUSCOUS

MOROCCO, ALGERIA, AND TUNISIA

Couscous is a pasta of North African origin. Made of small, dried particles of semolina, cooked couscous is very absorbent, making it the perfect foil for North African beef, chicken, or lamb tagines, or stews. The following recipe, made with vegetables, can easily be served as a hearty main course. Serve with a green salad or a refreshing Mediterranean orange salad (page 184).

2 tablespoons olive oil

2 leeks, washed well, white and light green parts only, sliced into thin rounds

3 large vine-ripened plum tomatoes, peeled, seeded, and coarsely chopped, or 3 canned plum tomatoes, seeded and coarsely chopped

2 medium carrots, peeled and cut into ³/₄-inch pieces

1 large turnip, peeled and cut into ¹/₂-inch dice

3 small zucchini, cut into ¹/₂-inch dice

1 large potato, peeled and cut into ³/₄-inch dice

2 stalks celery, cut into ¹/₂-inch dice

1¹/₂ cups cooked chickpeas (page 63) or one 19-ounce can chickpeas, drained and rinsed under water

1¹/₂ teaspoons ground cumin

1 teaspoon paprika

1 teaspoon salt

¹/₈ teaspoon freshly ground black pepper

3³/₄ cups Rich Vegetable Stock (page 46), Rich Chicken Stock (page 47), or canned broth

2 tablespoons olive oil

2 cups uncooked couscous

Heat the olive oil in the pressure cooker over medium-high heat. Add the leeks and sauté over low heat 3 to 4 minutes, or until soft. Stir frequently so that the leeks do not brown. Add the vegetables, chickpeas, cumin, paprika, salt, and black pepper. Cook over medium-high heat 2 minutes, stirring frequently. Add 1¹/₂ cups of the stock. Mix well.

Position the lid and lock in place. Raise the heat to high and bring to high pressure. Adjust the heat to stabilize the pressure and cook 3 minutes. Remove from the heat and lower the pressure using the cold-water-release method. Open the pressure cooker. Remove the vegetables from the pressure cooker with a slotted spoon to a large bowl. Cover and set aside. Pour the vegetable cooking liquid into a small saucepan and keep at a simmer, covered.

Pour the remaining stock into a medium-sized saucepan and bring to a boil. Add the olive oil and stir in the couscous. Bring to a boil, stirring constantly. Remove from heat and cover. Let sit 5 minutes. Fluff couscous with a fork.

Mound the couscous on a serving platter, forming a large well in the center. Place the cooked vegetables in the center of the well. Spoon the simmering reserved vegetable cooking liquid over the couscous and vegetables.

4 SERVINGS

APPROXIMATE NUTRITIONAL ANALYSIS PER SERVING

384 calories, 19g protein, 39g carbohydrates, 19g fat, 2mg cholesterol, 2026mg sodium

STUFFED VEGETABLES

Braised vegetables stuffed with savory fillings of rice, meat, and herbs are popular in both Greek and Turkish cooking.

5 tablespoons olive oil
1 large onion, chopped
$\frac{1}{2}$ cup long-grain rice
$\frac{1}{2}$ pound lean ground beef
$\frac{1}{4}$ cup canned, crushed tomatoes
1 cup water
$\frac{1}{4}$ cup chopped parsley
1 teaspoon chopped mint
1 teaspoon salt
$\frac{1}{8}$ teaspoon freshly ground black
   pepper

$\frac{1}{4}$ cup dried currants (optional)
2 medium-sized zucchini, cut in
   half lengthwise
4 small red peppers
2 medium-sized yellow onions
$\frac{1}{2}$ cup Rich Vegetable Stock (page
   46), Rich Beef Stock (page 48), or
   canned broth

Heat 3 tablespoons of the olive oil in the pressure cooker over medium-high heat. Add the chopped onion and sauté 4 to 5 minutes, or until soft. Stir frequently so that the onion does not brown. Add the rice. Cook 3 minutes, stirring constantly, or until the rice is translucent. Add the ground meat and brown, stirring to break up any large pieces. Add the tomatoes, water, parsley, mint, salt, and black pepper, and currants, if using. Stir to blend.

Position the lid and lock in place. Raise the heat to high and bring to high pressure. Adjust the heat to stabilize the pressure and cook 5 minutes. Remove from heat and lower pressure using the cold-water-release method. Open the pressure cooker. Taste and adjust for salt and black pepper. Place the stuffing mixture into a mixing bowl and let cool to room temperature.

Cut the ends off the zucchini. Using an apple corer or a thin-bladed paring knife, carefully hollow out the center, leaving a $\frac{1}{4}$-inch-thick shell. Slice the tops off the peppers and remove the seeds. Save the tops. Peel the onions and slice off the tops. Save the tops. Carefully scoop out the inside with a teaspoon or melon baller, leaving a $\frac{1}{2}$-inch-thick shell. Lightly sprinkle the inside of the vegetables with salt. Gently fill the vegetables with some of the stuffing mixture—do not pack. Cover the peppers and the onions with their tops and secure with toothpicks.

Heat the remaining 2 tablespoons olive oil in the pressure cooker over medium-high heat. In small batches, brown the stuffed vegetables on all sides just until they begin to take on some color. Place the browned peppers and onions upright in the pressure cooker. Lay the stuffed zucchini flat, between the other vegetables. Pour in the stock.

Position the lid on the pressure cooker and lock in place. Raise the heat to high and bring to high pressure. Adjust the heat to stabilize the pressure and cook 5 minutes. Remove from the heat and lower the pressure, using the cold-water-release method. Open the pressure cooker. Carefully remove the cooked stuffed vegetables with tongs or a large slotted spoon. Cut the onions in half. Pour some of the cooking liquid over the vegetables before serving.

4 SERVINGS

APPROXIMATE NUTRITIONAL ANALYSIS PER SERVING

440 calories, 18g protein, 40g carbohydrates, 25g fat, 36mg cholesterol, 863mg sodium

SAUTÉED MEDITERRANEAN VEGETABLES
Pisto Manchego

The French call it *ratatouille,* but in Spain it is known as *pisto manchego.* Hailing from La Mancha, the land of Don Quixote, located on the wind-swept plain of central Spain, this simple dish of sautéed vegetables is usually served with a fried egg or two on the side or perhaps with a grilled or fried pork chop.

¼ cup olive oil
1 large yellow onion, chopped
1 pound sweet Italian frying
   peppers, cored, seeded, and cut
   into thin strips
½ pound small potatoes, peeled
   and thinly sliced

1 pound small zucchini, peeled
   and cut into ¼-inch dice
½ cup tomato puree
¼ cup water
1½ teaspoons salt
⅛ teaspoon freshly ground black
   pepper

Heat the olive oil in the pressure cooker over medium-high heat. Add the onion and sauté 4 to 5 minutes or until the onion is soft. Stir frequently so that the onion does not brown. Add the peppers and potatoes and sauté 5 minutes over high heat stirring frequently. Add the zucchini and sauté 3 minutes. Stir in the tomato puree, water, salt, and black pepper.

Position the lid and lock in place. Raise the heat to high and bring to high pressure. Adjust the heat to stabilize the pressure and cook 6 minutes. Remove from heat and lower pressure using the cold-water-release method. Open the pressure cooker. Taste and adjust for salt and pepper.

4 SERVINGS

APPROXIMATE NUTRITIONAL ANALYSIS PER SERVING
241 calories, 4g protein, 29g carbohydrates, 14g fat, 0mg cholesterol, 933mg sodium

FISH AND SHELLFISH

The following cooking times are provided as guidelines to be used in cooking seafood in the pressure cooker. Cooking times can vary depending on the size of the individual pieces; maximum and minimum cooking times are given in some instances. When uncertain how long to cook something, always start with the shortest cooking time, since you can continue cooking for an additional couple of minutes until the desired texture is reached.

Since water and liquids boil more slowly at altitudes of more than 2,000 feet above sea level, the cooking time and the amount of cooking liquid must be increased accordingly. Please refer to page 28 for additional information.

All cooking times listed begin once high or maximum pressure is reached.

APPROXIMATE COOKING TIMES

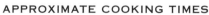

SEAFOOD	COOKING TIME	AMOUNT COOKING LIQUID
Clams, 1 to 1½ dozen	1 to 3 minutes	1 cup
Crabs, 1 to 2 pounds	2 to 3 minutes	1 cup
Lobster, 1½ to 2 pounds	2 to 3 minutes	1 cup
Mussels, 4 dozen small to medium	2 to 3 minutes	1 cup
Shrimp, 1 to 2 pounds	1 to 2 minutes	1 cup
Fish, whole, 1 to 2 pounds, gutted	5 to 6 minutes	1 cup
Fish steaks, 1½- to 2-inches thick	2 to 3 minutes	1 cup

FISH À LA CATAPLANA
Peixe na Cataplana

On my first trip and subsequent trips to Portimão in the Portuguese Algarve, I enjoyed a delicious fish stew that was prepared in a cooking utensil typical of the region, called a *cataplana*. The precursor of today's pressure cooker, the *cataplana*, which is made of hammered copper lined with tin, consists of two round, shallow, hinged halves in which food is braised. Since the *cataplana* does not have a top or bottom, so to speak, the entire vessel, which is locked when closed, is turned over in order to cook the fish evenly. The end result, as you can well imagine, is delicious.

Since you probably do not own a *cataplana*, I have adapted the basic recipe for *peixe na cataplana* to be made in the pressure cooker for equally excellent results.

6 tablespoons olive oil
2 large onions, thinly sliced
3 cloves garlic, peeled and minced
1 teaspoon paprika
1/8 teaspoon cayenne pepper
1 cup dry white wine
1 cup canned crushed tomatoes
1/2 cup finely chopped parsley
3 bay leaves, crumbled
1 1/2 teaspoons salt
1/4 teaspoon freshly ground black
pepper

2 pounds firm, white fish like
scrod, monkfish, or hake,
cleaned, deboned, and cut into
serving pieces
4-ounce slice Portuguese *presunto*
ham or Italian prosciutto,
coarsely chopped
2 medium-sized green peppers,
seeded and diced

Heat 4 tablespoons of the olive oil in the pressure cooker over medium-high heat. Add the onion and sauté 4 to 5 minutes, or until soft. Stir frequently so that the onion does not brown. Add the garlic, paprika, and cayenne pepper and sauté 1 minute. Pour in the wine and raise the heat to high. Bring to a boil. Once the alcohol has evaporated, in 1 or 2 minutes, add the tomatoes, parsley, bay leaves, salt, and black pepper.

Position the lid and lock in place. Bring to high pressure. Adjust the heat to stabilize the pressure and cook 3 minutes. Remove from heat and lower pressure using the cold-water-release method. Open the pressure cooker. Add the fish, ham, and diced green pepper and the remaining 2 tablespoons of olive oil. Stir well.

Position the lid and lock in place. Bring to high pressure over high heat. Adjust the heat to stabilize the pressure and cook 3 minutes. Remove from the heat and lower the pressure using the cold-water-release method. Open the pressure cooker. Taste and adjust for salt and pepper. Carefully remove the fish to a serving platter using a slotted spoon or a spatula. Spoon the sauce over the fish.

4 SERVINGS

APPROXIMATE NUTRITIONAL ANALYSIS PER SERVING

531 calories, 50g protein, 13g carbohydrates, 27g fat, 86mg cholesterol, 1364mg sodium

MUSSELS À LA CATAPLANA
Mexilhoes na Cataplana

In a addition to braising fish with tomatoes in a *cataplana* (page 129), the cooks of Portimão also prepare wonderful shellfish dishes using small clams or mussels that are steamed in their own juices along with some olive oil, citrus juice, and white wine.

Since it is almost impossible to obtain the tiny, thumbnail-sized clams found in the Algarve, this recipe uses mussels, but you can also use small littleneck or manilla clams. The only requisite for this recipe is to have plenty of good, crusty bread on hand, to sop up the delicious cooking liquid.

4 dozen small to medium-sized mussels (approximately 2 to 2¼ pounds), scrubbed well under cold water and debearded
1 cup cornmeal
¼ cup olive oil
3 cloves garlic, peeled and minced
4-ounce slice of Portuguese *presunto* or Italian prosciutto, coarsely chopped
⅔ cup dry white wine

2 tablespoons freshly squeezed orange juice
1 tablespoon freshly squeezed lemon juice
½ teaspoon salt
⅛ teaspoon freshly ground black pepper
2 tablespoons minced cilantro
2 tablespoons minced parsley

Place the mussels and cornmeal in a large bowl with enough cold water to cover. Soak for 1 hour. This will help the mussels release any sand they may contain. Rinse well in a colander under cold water.

Heat the olive oil in the pressure cooker over medium heat. Add the garlic and chopped *presunto* or prosciutto and sauté 1 minute. Add the white wine, orange and lemon juice, and salt and pepper. Raise the heat and bring to a boil. Stir in the mussels.

Position the lid and lock in place. Raise the heat to high and bring to high pressure. Adjust the heat to stabilize the pressure and cook 1 minute. Remove from the heat and lower the pressure using the cold-water-release method. Open the pressure cooker and stir in the minced cilantro and parsley. Discard any unopened mussels. Serve the mussels in large soup bowls with some of the cooking liquid.

4 SERVINGS

APPROXIMATE NUTRITIONAL ANALYSIS PER SERVING

411 calories, 36g protein, 12g carbohydrates, 21g fat, 85mg cholesterol, 1405mg sodium

FISH BRAISED IN GARLICKY TOMATO SAUCE
Pesce alla Pizzaiola

Alla pizzaiola is a common Neapolitan method for cooking meat or fish in garlicky tomato sauce. Pizzaiola owes its name to the fact that the sauce is very similar to that used in making another notable Neapolitan dish, pizza.

¼ cup olive oil
2 cloves garlic, peeled and crushed
3 cups canned crushed tomatoes
  (one 28-ounce can)
1 teaspoon dried oregano
1½ teaspoons salt
⅛ teaspoon freshly ground black
  pepper

2 teaspoons capers, drained and
  rinsed under water
2 pounds firm, white fish like
  monkfish, hake, or scrod,
  cleaned and cut into
  medium-sized pieces, about
  ½ to ¾ inch thick
2 teaspoons chopped parsley

Heat the olive oil in the pressure cooker over medium-high heat. Add the garlic and sauté just until golden. Add the tomatoes, oregano, salt, and black pepper. Bring to a simmer and let cook 5 minutes. Taste and adjust for salt and pepper. If the sauce tastes bitter, add ½ to 1 teaspoon of sugar. Add the capers.

With a large spoon, push aside some of the tomato sauce and place the fish on the bottom of the pressure cooker in a single layer, overlapping slightly if necessary. Spoon some of the sauce over the fish to cover.

Position the lid and lock in place. Raise the heat to high and bring to high pressure. Adjust the heat to stabilize the pressure and cook 3 minutes. Remove from the heat and lower the pressure using the cold-water-release method. Open the pressure cooker. With a spatula, carefully remove the cooked fish to a large serving platter. Cover the fish with the pizzaiola sauce and sprinkle with the chopped parsley.

4 SERVINGS

APPROXIMATE NUTRITIONAL ANALYSIS PER SERVING

393 calories, 44g protein, 13g carbohydrates, 18g fat, 73mg cholesterol, 1375mg sodium

PROVENÇAL POACHED SEAFOOD WITH GARLIC MAYONNAISE
Aïoli-Bourride

This nineteenth-century garlic-rich seafood dish from Provence is a wonderful combination of the many elements of the local cuisine: fish, shrimp, and mussels from the sea and white wine, olive oil, garlic, eggs, orange peel, and saffron from the fertile fields of the region. Together they provide a simple yet highly aromatic seafood stew seasoned with aïoli, the garlicky mayonnaise of the Midi.

³/₄ cup mayonnaise
2 tablespoons extra-virgin olive oil
2 cloves garlic, peeled and minced
2 cups Rich Fish Stock (page 49)
¹/₄ cup dry white wine
1 bay leaf
¹/₄ teaspoon fennel seeds
Strip of orange peel
1¹/₂ pounds firm white fish fillets
    like monkfish or hake, skin and
    bones removed, cut into chunks

2 threads saffron
¹/₂ pound large shrimp, peeled,
    deveined, with tails intact,
    rinsed under cold water
12 mussels, scrubbed well under
    cold water and debearded
1 tablespoon minced parsley
8 slices French bread, toasted

In a small saucepan, prepare the aïoli by whisking the mayonnaise, olive oil, and garlic, until well blended. Set aside.

Pour the fish stock and white wine into the pressure cooker along with the bay leaf, fennel seeds, and orange peel. Position the lid and lock in place. Place over high heat and bring to high pressure. Adjust the heat to stabilize the pressure and cook 5 minutes. Remove from the heat and lower the pressure using the cold-water-release method. Open the pressure cooker and strain the stock.

Return the stock to the pressure cooker and add the fish and saffron. Position the lid and lock in place. Bring to high pressure over high heat. Adjust the heat to stabilize the pressure and cook 3 minutes. Remove from the heat and lower the pressure using the cold-water-release method. Open the pressure cooker and remove the fish with a slotted spoon. Place the fish on a large, shallow platter and cover. Keep warm.

Add the shrimp and mussels to the broth and bring to a simmer over low heat.

Remove the shrimp with a slotted spoon after 2 to 3 minutes, or when they turn bright pink. Remove the mussels when they open. Set the shrimp and mussels aside in a bowl and cover. Keep warm.

Whisk one cup of the hot cooking liquid into the prepared aïoli in the saucepan. Bring to a slow simmer and continue beating with the whisk until the sauce is warmed through. Pour the aïoli sauce over the poached fish. Arrange the cooked shrimp and mussels on the platter and sprinkle with the minced parsley.

To serve, place two slices of the toasted French bread in each plate. Spoon some of the seafood and sauce on top. Serve with plain boiled potatoes.

4 SERVINGS

APPROXIMATE NUTRITIONAL ANALYSIS PER SERVING

1049 calories, 38g protein, 50g carbohydrates, 54g fat, 40mg cholesterol, 272mg sodium

MARINATED SQUID AND FENNEL SALAD

ITALY, SPAIN, AND GREECE

Squid—or calamari, as it is often known in this country—is a 10-armed member of the mollusk family. Treasured and featured in the cooking of most of the Mediterranean region, squid is commonly floured and deep-fried, stewed in its own ink, or enjoyed as in this recipe, prepared in a salad dressed simply with vinegar, olive oil, and herbs.

I particularly like the addition of fennel to this salad, since it adds an interesting contrast in both flavor and texture. If you prefer, you can substitute celery.

$3/4$ cup water
$1^1/2$ pounds squid, cleaned, body
    sacs cut into $1/4$-inch-thick rings
    and tentacles halved
$3/4$ cup extra-virgin olive oil
2 tablespoons red-wine vinegar
1 tablespoon lemon juice
2 cloves garlic, peeled and minced
1 teaspoon dried oregano

$1/2$ teaspoon salt
$1/4$ teaspoon freshly ground black
    pepper
2 small fennel bulbs, trimmed,
    quartered, and thinly sliced, or
    1 celery heart, cut diagonally
    into $1/8$-inch-thick slices

Pour the water into the pressure cooker. Place the pieces of squid in the steamer basket on the trivet in the pressure cooker. Position the lid and lock in place. Place over high heat and bring to high pressure. Cook $1^1/2$ minutes. Remove from the heat and lower the pressure using the cold-water-release method. Open the pressure cooker and carefully remove the steamer basket. Place the squid in a large serving bowl. Let cool to room temperature.

Prepare the vinaigrette by whisking together the olive oil, vinegar, lemon juice, garlic, oregano, salt, and black pepper. Add the fennel to the squid and toss with the vinaigrette. Cover and let the salad marinate in the refrigerator at least 4 hours before serving.

Taste and adjust for salt before serving

6 SERVINGS

APPROXIMATE NUTRITIONAL ANALYSIS PER SERVING
366 calories, 21g protein, 8g carbohydrates, 29g fat, 0mg cholesterol, 219mg sodium

TUNA STEAKS IN OLIVE OIL
Trancio di Tonnetto sott'Olio

The fishing of bluefin tuna off the Atlantic coast of Spain, near the Straits of Gibraltar, was first documented by the Phoenicians. Every spring, tens of thousands of tuna would enter the Mediterranean from the Atlantic on their way to spawning grounds in the Black Sea. Weighing between 500 to 1,000 pounds, the tuna would be harpooned and then filleted and salted. The ancient Romans were the first to seriously commercialize this industry by salting the tuna and preparing *garum*, a fermented paste not unlike anchovy paste, made from the tuna's organs and soft flesh.

When obtainable, fresh tuna was a gourmet's delight for the Romans, who prepared it simply with olive oil and salt, as documented by the Roman gourmet Archestratus in his treatise *High Living*: "Slice it and roast it all rightly, sprinkling just a little of salt, and buttering it with oil. Eat the slices hot, dipping them into a sauce piquant; they are nice even if you want to eat them plain, like deathless gods in form and stature" (Athenaeus 7.303).

While the following recipe from Italy steams the tuna rather than roasts it, it is not unlike that described by Archestratus. Serve this dish as part of an antipasto or an entrée for lunch or supper on a hot summer's day.

⅔ cup extra-virgin olive oil	1 cup water
2 cloves garlic, peeled and crushed	2 pounds tuna steaks,
2 tablespoons coarsely chopped	approximately ¾ to 1 inch thick
parsley	2 teaspoons minced parsley
4 bay leaves, crumbled	1 lemon, cut into 4 wedges
2 teaspoons salt	
Pinch crushed, hot red pepper	
flakes	

One hour before steaming the tuna, prepare the marinade. In a small bowl, mix together the olive oil, garlic, parsley, bay leaves, salt, and red pepper. Set aside.

Pour the water into the pressure cooker. Lightly grease the steaming basket with vegetable oil. Place as many tuna steaks in the basket as can fit in a single layer without overlapping. It will be necessary to steam the tuna in two batches. Place the steamer basket on the trivet.

Position the lid and lock in place. Place over high heat and bring to high pressure.

Adjust the heat to stabilize the pressure and cook 3 minutes. Remove from the heat and lower the pressure using the cold-water-release method. Open the pressure cooker. Carefully remove the steamer basket. Repeat with the remaining tuna.

Place the steamed tuna steaks on a shallow platter just large enough to hold them. With a long-tined fork, prick the steamed tuna a few times, taking care not to break it. Pour the marinade through a small strainer over the tuna. Press on the herbs and spices with the back of a spoon to extract all the marinade. Let the tuna marinate at room temperature at least 2 hours before serving, spooning some of the marinade over the tuna every 10 to 15 minutes. The tuna will gradually absorb most of the marinade.

When serving, spoon a small amount of the marinade on each plate. Place the tuna on the plates and spoon any remaining marinade on top. Sprinkle with the minced parsley and serve with lemon wedges.

4 SERVINGS

APPROXIMATE NUTRITIONAL ANALYSIS PER SERVING

650 calories, 53g protein, 2g carbohydrates, 47g fat, 86mg cholesterol, 1156mg sodium

MEAT AND POULTRY

The following cooking times are provided as guidelines to be used in cooking meat and poultry in the pressure cooker. Cooking times can vary depending on the quality of the meat and poultry, as well as the size of the individual pieces; maximum and minimum cooking times are given in some instances. When uncertain how long to cook something, always start with the shortest cooking time, since you can always continue cooking for an additional couple of minutes until the desired texture is reached.

Since water and liquids boil more slowly at altitudes over 2,000 feet above sea level, the cooking time and the amount of cooking liquid needed must be increased accordingly. Please refer to page 28 for additional information.

All cooking times listed begin once high or maximum pressure is reached.

APPROXIMATE COOKING TIMES

MEAT AND POULTRY	COOKING TIME	AMOUNT COOKING LIQUID
Beef/Veal, roast or brisket, 3 pounds	35 to 40 minutes	1½ cups
Beef/Veal, shanks, 1½-inches thick	25 to 30 minutes	1 cup
Beef/Veal, 1½ pounds, 1-inch cubes	10 to 15 minutes	1 cup
Beef, corned, 3 pounds	50 to 60 minutes	2 cups
Meatballs, up to 2 pounds, browned	8 to 10 minutes	1 cup
Pork, roast, 3 pounds	40 to 45 minutes	1½ cups
Pork, ribs, 2 pounds	15 to 20 minutes	1½ cups
Pork, smoked butt, 2 pounds	20 to 25 minutes	1½ cups
Pork, ham shank, 3 pounds	30 minutes	1½ cups
Lamb, 1½ pounds, 1-inch cubes	10 to 15 minutes	1 cup
Lamb, leg, 3 pounds	35 to 40 minutes	1½ cups
Chicken, whole, 2 to 3 pounds	15 to 20 minutes	1 cup
Chicken, pieces, 2 to 3 pounds	8 to 10 minutes	¾ cup
Cornish hens, 2	8 to 10 minutes	¾ cup

BEEF BOURGUIGNON
Boeuf à la Bourguignonne

This most classic of all French beef stews is prepared in a red-wine sauce accompanied by bacon, mushrooms, and braised onions. It is best prepared the day before you wish to serve it to allow the flavors to develop.

Marinated meat:

3 cups dry red wine
2 cloves garlic, peeled and minced
1/2 teaspoon dried thyme
1/4 teaspoon dried rosemary
1 teaspoon salt
1/4 teaspoon freshly ground black pepper
2 pounds boneless beef chuck, trimmed of all fat and cut into 1 1/2-inch cubes

4 tablespoons unbleached all-purpose flour
1 teaspoon salt
1/4 teaspoon freshly ground black pepper
3 tablespoons olive oil
3/4 pound pearl onions, peeled
3 strips bacon, coarsely chopped
8 ounces white button mushrooms, wiped clean and trimmed
1 tablespoon minced parsley

Combine the marinade ingredients in a large nonreactive bowl. Add the beef and mix well. Cover and refrigerate at least 4 hours or overnight. Remove the meat from the marinade and pat dry with paper towels. Reserve 2 cups of the marinade.

Combine the flour, salt, and black pepper in a shallow bowl. Dredge the meat in the flour mixture, shaking off any excess.

Heat the olive oil in the pressure cooker over high heat. Brown the meat on all sides in small batches. Remove the browned pieces to a dish and set aside. Reduce the heat to low and sauté the onions and bacon 2 to 3 minutes, or until the bacon just begins to brown, stirring frequently so that the onions do not burn. Add the browned meat along with any collected juices, the mushrooms, and the reserved marinade.

Position the lid and lock in place. Raise the heat to high and bring to high pressure. Adjust the heat to stabilize the pressure and cook 20 minutes. Remove from the heat and lower the pressure using the cold-water-release method. Open the pressure cooker. Taste and adjust for salt and pepper. Stir in the parsley.

6 SERVINGS

APPROXIMATE NUTRITIONAL ANALYSIS PER SERVING

614 calories, 33g protein, 13g carbohydrates, 39g fat, 111mg cholesterol, 1065mg sodium

BEEF STEW FROM PROVENCE
Daube Provençale de Boeuf

Fragrant with the flavors of Provence, this beef stew is a delicious departure from other stews. Although the ingredient list is long, do not be put off; it only takes a few minutes to assemble everything. The resulting gravy is wonderful served over egg noodles or boiled potatoes.

Marinated meat:

1 large onion, coarsely chopped
1 large carrot, peeled and coarsely
   chopped
1 stalk celery, coarsely chopped
2 cloves garlic, peeled and
   coarsely chopped
1 cup dry red wine
2 tablespoons olive oil
1 strip orange zest
1/4 teaspoon dried thyme
2 bay leaves, crumbled
1/2 teaspoon coarsely ground black
   pepper
2 pounds boneless beef chuck,
   trimmed of all fat and cut into
   2-inch cubes

4 tablespoons unbleached
   all-purpose flour
1 teaspoon salt
1/4 teaspoon freshly ground black
   pepper
3 tablespoons olive oil
1 large onion, finely chopped
6 large carrots, peeled, cut in half
   and then into 1-inch-long pieces
1 cup canned crushed tomatoes
1/4 cup oil-cured black olives
   (optional)
2 teaspoons salt
1/4 teaspoon freshly ground black
   pepper
2 tablespoons minced parsley

Mix the marinade ingredients together in a large nonreactive bowl. Add the beef and mix well. Cover and refrigerate at least 4 hours or overnight. Remove the meat from the marinade and pat dry with paper towels. Pour the marinade through a fine-mesh strainer. Discard the vegetables and seasonings. Set the strained marinade aside.

Combine the flour, salt, and black pepper in a shallow bowl. Dredge the meat in the flour mixture, shaking off any excess. Heat the olive oil in the pressure cooker over high heat. Brown the beef on all sides in small batches. Remove the browned pieces and set aside in a bowl. Reduce the heat to low and sauté the onion 4 to 5 minutes, or until soft. Stir frequently so that the onion does not brown. Add the browned meat along with any collected juices. Add the carrots, crushed tomatoes, olives if desired, salt, black pepper, and reserved marinade.

Position the lid and lock in place. Raise the heat to high and bring to high pressure. Adjust the heat to stabilize the pressure and cook 20 minutes. Remove from heat and lower the pressure using the cold-water-release method. Open the pressure cooker. Taste and adjust for salt and pepper. Stir in the parsley.

6 SERVINGS

APPROXIMATE NUTRITIONAL ANALYSIS PER SERVING

597 calories, 31g protein, 22g carbohydrates, 40g fat, 103mg cholesterol, 1017mg sodium

BEEF OLIVES

Malta is the only English-speaking country in the Mediterranean and probably the least well known of the region. Now an independent nation, Malta was inhabited over the centuries by the Phoenicians, Greeks, Carthaginians, Romans, Arabs, Normans, and the British, under whose control it remained until 1964.

Culinarily speaking, Maltese cooking shares many common elements with that of its closest neighbor, Sicily. In fact, the following recipe for beef olives (so called because they resemble large olives) is quite similar to the Sicilian dish of rolled, braised beef, *farsumagro*.

4 tablespoons olive oil	4 very thin slices filet of beef,
1 large onion, chopped	trimmed of all fat, about
2 cloves garlic, peeled and minced	1½ pounds
8 ounces ground lean pork	1 medium carrot, peeled and
1½ teaspoons salt	minced
¼ teaspoon freshly ground black	1 stalk celery, minced
pepper	½ cup dry red wine
1 teaspoon minced parsley	1 cup canned crushed tomatoes
¼ teaspoon dried marjoram	1 teaspoon salt
2 large hard-boiled eggs, peeled	¼ teaspoon freshly ground black
and mashed with a fork	pepper

Heat 2 tablespoons of the olive oil in the pressure cooker over medium-high heat. Add the onion and garlic and sauté 4 to 5 minutes, or until the onion is soft. Stir frequently so the onion does not brown. Remove half the onion-and-garlic mixture and set aside. Add the ground pork, ½ teaspoon of the salt, ⅛ teaspoon of the black pepper, the parsley, and the marjoram to the onion mixture in the pressure cooker and sauté just until the meat loses its pink color. Remove from the pressure cooker to a mixing bowl and mix in the mashed egg. Spread ¼ of the mixture in the center of each slice of beef. Roll up lengthwise, tucking in the sides. Securely tie up the beef rolls with kitchen string.

Heat the remaining 2 tablespoons olive oil in the pressure cooker over high heat. Brown the beef rolls on all sides. Add the reserved onion-and-garlic mixture and the chopped carrots, celery, and red wine. Bring the wine to a boil. Once the alcohol has evaporated, about 1 to 2 minutes, stir in the tomatoes, salt, and black pepper. Position the lid and lock in place. Bring to high pressure. Adjust the heat to stabilize the pressure and cook 5 minutes. Remove from the heat and lower the pressure using the cold-water-release method. Open the pressure cooker. Taste and adjust for salt and pepper.

4 SERVINGS

APPROXIMATE NUTRITIONAL ANALYSIS PER SERVING

575 calories, 49g protein, 9g carbohydrates, 35g fat, 248mg cholesterol, 1569mg sodium

MIXED BOIL WITH THREE SAUCES
Bollito Misto ai Tre Salsa

Do not be put off by the name of this recipe. Bollito misto is a lot more than just boiled meats on a plate. Traditionally prepared in the largest stockpot possible, bollito misto can contain a variety of cuts and kinds of meat including beef, veal, chicken, calf's head, tongue, and sausages, along with root vegetables. Slow-cooked in stock, the meats are sliced and served with the vegetables accompanied by at least three different types of sauces. The broth is strained and served as a first course with small pasta or tortellini.

I have limited the number of meats to just three in the following recipe: a piece of beef, a chicken breast, and some sausage. Recipes for the three sauces represent the colors of the Italian flag: green, white, and red.

8 cups Rich Beef Stock (page 48), or canned beef broth

3 large leeks, split, rinsed well, and cut into 3-inch-long pieces

4 large carrots, peeled and cut into chunks

4 medium-sized potatoes, peeled and quartered

1 pound garlic sausage (*cotechino*, available at some Italian markets; if unavailable, use fresh, unsmoked, Polish *kielbasa* or other garlic sausage)

1½ pounds bottom round of beef

1 split chicken breast, about 1 pound

1 teaspoon salt

8 ounces cheese- or meat-filled tortellini, cooked until tender

Pour the beef stock into the pressure cooker. Add the vegetables and sausage. Position the lid and lock in place. Place over high heat and bring to high pressure. Adjust the heat to stabilize the pressure and cook 4 minutes. Remove from the heat and lower the pressure using the cold-water-release method. Open the pressure cooker. Using a slotted spoon remove the vegetables and sausage to a bowl. Cover and set aside.

Add the beef to the stock. Bring to a boil. Skim off any scum with a slotted spoon. Once the stock begins to boil clear, position the lid on the pressure cooker and lock in place. Raise the heat to high and bring to high pressure. Adjust the heat to stabilize the pressure and cook 25 minutes. Remove from the heat and release the pressure using the cold-water-release method.

Add the chicken to the beef and stock. Reposition the lid, lock in place, and bring to high pressure. Adjust the pressure and cook under high pressure an additional 20 minutes.

Remove from the heat and let the pressure drop naturally. Open the pressure cooker. Taste and adjust for salt. Add the cooked vegetables and sausage. Let sit for a few minutes until they are warmed through.

Thinly slice the beef and chicken and place on a large serving platter, along with the vegetables and sausages. Spoon some of the hot broth over the meats and vegetables to moisten. Cover to keep warm.

Serve the tortellini in the broth as a first course. Serve the meats and vegetables with the sauces that follow.

6 SERVINGS

APPROXIMATE NUTRITIONAL ANALYSIS PER SERVING WITHOUT PASTA AND SAUCES

690 calories, 57g protein, 35g carbohydrates, 35g fat, 204mg cholesterol, 2467 mg sodium

Green Sauce

◆ *Salsa Verde*

⅔ cup Italian parsley leaves, packed	1 clove garlic, peeled and minced
2½ tablespoons capers	1 teaspoon red-wine vinegar
	½ cup extra-virgin olive oil

Place all of the ingredients in a blender jar and process on low until smooth. Do not liquefy. Spoon into a small serving bowl.

6 SERVINGS

APPROXIMATE NUTRITIONAL ANALYSIS PER SERVING

163 calories, 0g protein, 0g carbohydrates, 18g fat, 0mg cholesterol, 104mg sodium

White Horseradish Sauce

◆ *Salsina di Barbaforte*

¼ cup prepared horseradish	1 teaspoon white-wine vinegar
½ cup extra-virgin olive oil	½ teaspoon salt

Place all the ingredients in a blender jar and process on low until smooth. Spoon into a small serving bowl.

6 SERVINGS

APPROXIMATE NUTRITIONAL ANALYSIS PER SERVING

163 calories, 0g protein, 1g carbohydrates, 18g fat, 0mg cholesterol, 187mg sodium

Red Sauce

◆ *Salsa Rossa*

¹/₄ cup olive oil
2 large onions, thinly sliced
2 large red peppers, halved, cored,
   seeded, and cut into
   ¹/₄-inch-thick slices

2 cups canned crushed tomatoes
1 teaspoon salt
¹/₈ teaspoon freshly ground black
   pepper

Heat the olive oil over medium-high heat in a medium-sized saucepan. Add the onion and sauté 4 to 5 minutes, or until soft. Stir frequently so that the onion does not brown. Add the red peppers and sauté 5 to 6 minutes, or until soft, stirring frequently. Add the crushed tomatoes, salt, and black pepper. Stir well. Simmer 20 minutes, stirring periodically. Taste and adjust for salt and pepper. Spoon into a small serving bowl. Serve hot.

6 SERVINGS

APPROXIMATE NUTRITIONAL ANALYSIS PER SERVING

125 calories, 2g protein, 11g carbohydrates, 9g fat, 0mg cholesterol, 488mg sodium

NEAPOLITAN BEEF RAGÙ
Ragù alla Napoletana

Ragù alla napoletana is the classic tomato sauce from southern Italy. It is traditionally simmered for close to 2 hours, but the pressure cooker does an admirable job in only a fraction of a time.

Serve this sauce over cooked dried macaroni, or use it to make baked pasta dishes like lasagne. Serve the meat sliced as the second course of the meal, along with a green salad.

3 tablespoons olive oil
2 pounds beef bottom round,
    trimmed of all visible fat
1 large onion, minced
2 large carrots, peeled and
    minced
½ cup dry red wine
2 tablespoons tomato paste

6 cups canned plum tomatoes
    (two 28-ounce cans) with juice,
    strained in a food mill
1 teaspoon sugar
4 teaspoons salt
1 teaspoon freshly ground black
    pepper

Heat the olive oil in the pressure cooker over high heat. Add the meat and brown evenly on all sides. Remove the browned meat and set aside. Reduce the heat to medium-high and sauté the onion 4 to 5 minutes, or until soft. Stir frequently so that the onion does not brown. Add the carrots and sauté 2 minutes, stirring constantly. Pour in the wine and raise the heat to high. Bring to a boil. Once the alcohol has evaporated, about 1 to 2 minutes, add the tomato paste. Stir well to blend. Add the strained tomatoes, sugar, salt, and black pepper. Stir well. Add the browned beef and any collected juices.

Position the lid and lock in place. Raise the heat to high and bring to high pressure. Adjust the heat to stabilize the pressure and cook 30 minutes. Remove from the heat and let the pressure drop naturally. Open the pressure cooker. Taste and adjust the sauce for salt and pepper.

6 SERVINGS

APPROXIMATE NUTRITIONAL ANALYSIS PER SERVING

359 calories, 34g protein, 16g carbohydrates, 17g fat, 93mg cholesterol, 1917mg sodium

MEATBALLS WITH PEAS
Albondigas en Salsa

Meatballs appear throughout the cooking of the Mediterranean basin in numerous variations. Making meatballs is a way to extend a small amount of meat by adding bread and other fillers. They can be made with beef, veal, pork, or lamb, depending on their country of origin. While we usually associate meatballs with spaghetti, in the Mediterranean region they stand on their own as an entrée.

Spanish meatballs with peas is not unlike a stew. Cooked in a wine-enriched tomato-and-vegetable sauce with peas, these meatballs are traditionally served with thin-cut, fried potatoes.

Meatballs:

4 slices day-old white bread, crusts removed
¼ cup milk
¾ pound lean ground beef
¾ pound lean ground pork
2 large eggs
3 cloves garlic, peeled and minced
1½ tablespoons minced parsley

1½ teaspoons salt
⅛ teaspoon freshly ground black pepper
Flour for dredging
Vegetable oil for frying

Sauce:

2 tablespoons olive oil
1 large onion, finely chopped
1 large carrot, finely chopped
1 large vine-ripened tomato, peeled, seeded, and coarsely chopped, or 3 canned plum tomatoes, seeded and coarsely chopped

2 teaspoons flour
½ cup dry white wine
1¾ cups Rich Beef Stock (page 48) or canned broth
1 cup fresh or frozen green peas
Salt to taste
Freshly ground black pepper to taste

Prepare the meatballs by tearing the bread into small pieces. Combine with the milk in a large mixing bowl. Soak until soft. Add the remaining ingredients and mix together. Shape into 24 small meatballs. Dredge in flour.

In a large skillet, heat ½ inch of vegetable oil over medium-high heat. Add the meatballs and fry in batches, turning to lightly brown on all sides. Remove with a slotted spoon and drain on paper towels.

Prepare the sauce by heating the olive oil in the pressure cooker over medium-high heat. Add the onion and sauté 4 to 5 minutes, or until soft. Stir frequently so that the onion does not brown. Add the carrot and tomato. Cook 2 minutes, stirring continuously. Sprinkle the vegetables with the flour and stir to blend. Add the white wine and stock. Stir well. Add the meatballs and stir to cover with sauce.

Position the lid and lock in place. Raise the heat to high and bring to high pressure. Cook 8 minutes. Remove from the heat and lower the pressure using the cold-water-release method. Open the pressure cooker and stir in the peas. Reposition the lid on the pressure cooker and lock in place. Over high heat bring the pressure cooker to high pressure. Once high pressure is reached, immediately remove from heat and lower the pressure using the cold-water-release method. Taste and adjust for salt and pepper. Serve over thin-cut fried potatoes, if desired.

6 SERVINGS

APPROXIMATE NUTRITIONAL ANALYSIS PER SERVING

699 calories, 34g protein, 67g carbohydrates, 30g fat, 147mg cholesterol, 1297mg sodium

VEAL STEW WITH RED PEPPERS
Axox d'Espelette

BASQUE REGION, SPAIN AND FRANCE

The Basque regions of Spain and France are inhabited by the descendants of early inhabitants of the Iberian Peninsula. To this day Basques maintain their own language and customs, which are remarkably distinct from those of their Spanish and French neighbors.

Basque cooking is characterized by rich, flavorful sauces in which meat, poultry, and fish are braised, as in the following veal stew with sweet red peppers.

1/4 cup unbleached all-purpose
   flour
1 teaspoon salt
1/8 teaspoon freshly ground black
   pepper
1/8 teaspoon cayenne pepper
2 pounds veal stew meat, trimmed
   of all visible fat and cut into
   1-inch cubes

3 tablespoons olive oil
1 large onion, peeled, cut in half,
   and thinly sliced
2 cloves garlic, peeled and minced
4 large red peppers, cored, seeded,
   and cut into thin strips
1 cup Rich Chicken Stock (page
   47), or canned chicken broth

Combine the flour, salt, and the black and cayenne peppers in a shallow bowl. Dredge the meat in the flour mixture, shaking off any excess.

Heat the oil in the pressure cooker over high heat. Brown the meat on all sides, in small batches. Remove the browned pieces of meat and set aside. Reduce the heat to low and sauté the onion and garlic 4 to 5 minutes, or until soft. Stir frequently so that the onion does not brown. Add the red peppers and sauté 2 minutes. Add the browned meat and any collected juices from the dish. Pour in the stock. Stir well.

Position the lid and lock in place. Raise the heat and bring to high pressure. Adjust the heat to stabilize the pressure. Cook 12 minutes. Remove from the heat and release the pressure using the cold-water-release method. Open the pressure cooker. Taste and adjust for salt. Serve with boiled potatoes or noodles, if desired.

4 SERVINGS

APPROXIMATE NUTRITIONAL ANALYSIS PER SERVING
551 calories, 44g protein, 18g carbohydrates, 34g fat, 175mg cholesterol, 1160mg sodium

BRAISED VEAL SHANKS
Osso Buco

Osso buco, a specialty of Milan, means "hollow bone." This refers to the opening of the shank bone once the marrow is extracted and eaten. The osso buco is slow-braised in a tomato-wine sauce to the point where the meat falls off the bone. For an authentic pairing, start your dinner off with another Milanese favorite, *risotto alla milanese,* page 87.

¼ cup unbleached all-purpose
    flour
½ teaspoon salt
¼ teaspoon freshly ground black
    pepper
4 large veal shanks, 1½ inches
    thick
3 tablespoons olive oil
1 medium onion, finely chopped
3 garlic cloves, peeled and
    minced
½ cup canned plum tomatoes,
    drained, seeded, and chopped

½ cup dry white wine
½ teaspoon dried basil
½ teaspoon dried oregano
1 teaspoon salt
⅛ teaspoon freshly ground black
    pepper
½ cup Rich Beef Stock (page 48),
    or canned broth
¼ cup minced parsley
Grated zest of one lemon

In a large shallow bowl, mix together the flour, salt, and black pepper. Trim any visible fat from the veal shanks and dredge in the seasoned flour. Heat the olive oil in the pressure cooker over medium-high heat. Brown the veal shanks on both sides, two at a time. Remove when browned and set aside. Add the onion and garlic and sauté over low heat 4 to 5 minutes, or until soft. Stir frequently so that the onion does not brown. Add the tomatoes, white wine, dried basil, oregano, salt, and black pepper. Raise heat and let boil 1 to 2 minutes, or until the alcohol in the wine evaporates, about 1 to 2 minutes. Stir in the beef stock. Add the browned veal shanks and any collected juices from the dish.

Position the lid and lock in place. Raise the heat to high and bring to high pressure. Adjust the heat to stabilize the pressure and cook 20 minutes. Remove from heat and lower pressure using the cold-water-release method. Open the pressure cooker. Place the cooked veal shanks on a large serving platter. Taste the sauce and adjust for salt and pepper. Spoon some sauce over the meat. Sprinkle with the parsley and grated lemon zest.

4 SERVINGS

APPROXIMATE NUTRITIONAL ANALYSIS PER SERVING
391 calories, 26g protein, 11g carbohydrates, 7g fat, 95mg cholesterol, 1015mg sodium

POACHED VEAL WITH PIQUANT TUNA MAYONNAISE
Vitello Tonnato

This is perhaps one of the most elegant and easiest-to-prepare cold entrées that I know. I first enjoyed vitello tonnato at a café in Milan's Galleria, an enclosed pedestrian shopping area. Do not be put off by the combination of flavors. You will be pleasantly surprised when you taste how deliciously the tuna mayonnaise blends with the poached veal.

The rich stock that results from poaching the veal should be saved for later use, perhaps as a simple broth with tortellini or cappelletti, small Italian stuffed pastalike dumplings

2 pounds lean veal roast, firmly trussed
1 medium carrot, peeled and coarsely chopped
1 stalk celery, coarsely chopped
1 medium onion, coarsely chopped
1 bay leaf
Water to cover meat
1 (7-ounce) can tuna, packed in oil, preferably olive oil, undrained

2 teaspoons freshly squeezed lemon juice
1/4 cup extra-virgin olive oil
2 tablespoons capers, rinsed under cold water
1 cup mayonnaise
Lemon slices; whole parsley leaves; slivered, oil-cured black olives; and capers, for garnish

Place the veal roast, carrots, celery, onion, and bay leaf in the pressure cooker. Pour in just enough water to cover the meat. Do not fill the pressure cooker more than two-thirds full. Position the lid and lock in place. Place over high heat and bring to high pressure. Adjust the heat to stabilize the pressure and cook 45 minutes. Remove from heat and let pressure drop naturally. Open the pressure cooker and let the meat cool to room temperature in the stock.

While the meat cools, prepare the tuna mayonnaise. Place the tuna, lemon juice, olive oil, and capers in the bowl of a food processor or a blender jar. Process until creamy and smooth. Slowly fold the tuna mixture into the mayonnaise in a large bowl. Cover and refrigerate until ready to use.

When the meat is cool, remove from the stock and place on a cutting board. Remove the trussing strings and cut the veal into thin slices. Strain the stock and reserve for another use.

Spread some of the tuna mayonnaise over the bottom of a serving platter. Cover with a layer of the sliced veal. Cover the veal slices with the tuna mayonnaise. Repeat layering the meat and the mayonnaise, ending with mayonnaise. Cover with plastic wrap and refrigerate at least 4 hours or overnight.

Bring to room temperature before serving. Garnish with lemon slices, parsley leaves, sliced black olives, and capers.

6 MAIN-COURSE SERVINGS OR 12 APPETIZER SERVINGS

APPROXIMATE NUTRITIONAL ANALYSIS PER MAIN-COURSE SERVING

626 calories, 37g protein, 1g carbohydrates, 52g fat, 137mg cholesterol, 428mg sodium

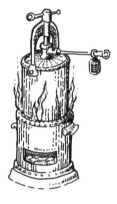

VEAL STEW WITH EGGPLANT

TURKEY

Because Turkey straddles Europe and Asia, the influence of Turkish cuisine, a mixture of Byzantine and Oriental cooking styles, was felt throughout the rest of the region during centuries of Ottoman rule.

This savory stew combines the Western and Eastern influences of this country in one dish: veal and tomatoes from Europe and eggplant from Asia.

1 large eggplant, approximately
  1½ pounds, peeled and cut into
  ½-inch cubes
Salt
¼ cup olive oil
1½ pounds veal stew meat,
  trimmed of all visible fat and
  cut into 1-inch cubes

1 large onion, finely chopped
1 cup canned tomato puree
½ cup water
½ teaspoon ground cumin
¼ teaspoon ground allspice
1 teaspoon salt
1 tablespoon minced parsley

Place the eggplant in a large colander and sprinkle lightly with salt. Let sit one hour to drain. Press on the eggplant to remove any excess liquid.

Heat the olive oil in the pressure cooker over high heat. Add the meat and brown evenly on all sides. Remove and set aside. Lower the heat to low and sauté the onion 4 to 5 minutes, or until soft. Stir frequently so that the onion does not brown. Add the drained eggplant and sauté 2 minutes. Return the browned meat to the pressure cooker along with any collected juices. Add the tomato puree, water, cumin, allspice, and salt. Cook 2 minutes, stirring frequently.

Position the lid and lock in place. Raise the heat to high and bring to high pressure. Adjust the heat to stabilize the pressure and cook 15 minutes. Remove from the heat and lower the pressure using the cold-water-release method. Taste and adjust for salt. Stir in the minced parsley before serving.

4 SERVINGS

APPROXIMATE NUTRITIONAL ANALYSIS PER SERVING
470 calories, 31g protein, 19g carbohydrates, 31g fat, 131mg cholesterol, 899mg sodium

PORK WITH CLAMS ALENTEJO-STYLE
Porco Alentejana

The Alentejo province of Portugal stretches from the Atlantic coast to the Spanish border, occupying almost one-third of Portugal. Known as the bread basket of Portugal because of its vast plains of wheat, the Alentejo is also known for its wonderful cuisine.

The first time I visited Portugal, we entered by way of Alentejo through the walled city of Elvas on the Spanish border. Besides the historical beauty of the city and its ancient aqueduct, Elvas is known for its cuisine, especially *porco alentejana*, this interesting dish that combines marinated pork with clams in a rich, flavorful sauce.

Marinated pork:

$^2/_3$ cup dry white wine
1 tablespoon olive oil
1 clove garlic, peeled and
   minced
1 bay leaf, crumbled
1 teaspoon salt
1 tablespoon paprika
$1^1/_2$ pounds boneless pork
   tenderloin, trimmed of all fat
   and cut into $1^1/_2$-inch cubes

3 tablespoons olive oil
1 large onion, chopped
1 clove garlic, peeled and minced
1 tablespoon tomato paste
$^1/_2$ teaspoon salt
$^1/_8$ teaspoon freshly ground black
   pepper
$^1/_3$ cup water
18 small littleneck clams, scrubbed
   well under cold water

Mix the marinade ingredients together in a large nonreactive bowl. Add the pork and mix well. Cover with a plate and refrigerate overnight.

The next day, remove the pork from the marinade with a slotted spoon and pat dry. Pour the marinade through a fine-mesh strainer and set aside.

Heat the olive oil in the pressure cooker over high heat. Brown the pork on all sides in small batches. Remove the browned meat and set aside. Reduce the heat to low and sauté the onion and garlic 4 to 5 minutes, or until soft. Stir frequently so the onion does not brown. Add the tomato paste, salt, and black pepper. Stir to blend. Stir in the reserved marinade and water. Add the browned pork along with any of the collected juices. Stir well.

Position the lid and lock in place. Raise the heat to high and bring to high pressure. Adjust the heat to stabilize the pressure and cook 12 minutes. Remove from heat and lower pressure using the cold-water-release method. Open the pressure cooker. Taste and adjust for salt and pepper.

Place the clams on top of the cooked pork. Position the lid on the pressure cooker and lock in place. Raise the heat to high and bring to high pressure. Adjust the heat to stabilize the pressure and cook 1 minute. Remove from the heat and lower the pressure using the cold-water-release method. Open the pressure cooker. Discard any unopened clams. Serve with thin-cut fried or boiled potatoes.

4 SERVINGS

APPROXIMATE NUTRITIONAL ANALYSIS PER SERVING

464 calories, 43g protein, 7g carbohydrates, 26g fat, 116mg cholesterol, 923mg sodium

LOIN OF PORK WITH BITTER-ORANGE SAUCE
Lomo a la Naranja

The first oranges that were brought back to Europe from Asia were bitter oranges. Known for their fragrant blossoms and aromatic fruit, these predecessors of today's eating and juice oranges decorate Spanish streets and are used in place of tart lemons when preparing marinades.

Since bitter oranges are usually only available during certain times of the year at Hispanic food markets (sold as *naranjas agrias*) you can easily substitute freshly squeezed orange and lime juice to come up with a close approximation of tartness and citrus flavor.

3 tablespoons olive oil

2 pounds boneless pork tenderloin, trimmed of all visible fat and cut into 1½-inch cubes

1 large onion, peeled and thinly sliced

4 large cloves garlic, peeled and minced

¾ cup freshly squeezed orange juice

2 tablespoons freshly squeezed lime juice

1 teaspoon salt

¼ teaspoon freshly ground black pepper

1 teaspoon dried oregano

1 teaspoon ground cumin

1 bay leaf, crumbled

Heat the oil in the pressure cooker over high heat. Brown the pork on all sides in two batches. Place the browned pork in a large dish and set aside. Lower the heat. Add the onion and garlic and sauté 4 to 5 minutes or until the onion is soft. Stir frequently so that the onion does not brown. Add the orange and lime juices and the remaining ingredients. Bring to a boil. Add the browned pork along with any collected juices.

Position the lid and lock in place. Raise the heat to high and bring to high pressure. Adjust the heat to stabilize the pressure and cook 12 minutes. Lower the pressure using the cold-water-release method. Open the pressure cooker. Over high heat, bring the cooking liquid to a boil and let reduce until thick. Taste and adjust for salt and pepper.

4 SERVINGS

APPROXIMATE NUTRITIONAL ANALYSIS PER SERVING

486 calories, 50g protein, 10g carbohydrates, 26g fat, 136mg cholesterol, 622mg sodium

STUFFED PORK BUNDLES
Involtini di Maiale

These delicious pork bundles from the Italian island of Sardinia are stuffed with a savory filling of bread and cheese. Highly addictive, they are, fortunately, quick and easy to make.

6 slices good-quality white bread
1 large egg, lightly beaten
1/4 cup freshly grated Pecorino
   Romano cheese
2 teaspoons minced parsley
1 clove garlic, peeled and minced
12 very thin slices boneless loin of
   pork, trimmed of all fat and
   pounded flat (about 1 1/2 pounds)

3 tablespoons olive oil
1 small onion, sliced thinly
1/2 teaspoon salt
Pinch freshly ground black pepper
1/2 cup dry white wine

Tear the bread into small pieces and place in a mixing bowl. Add the beaten egg, the grated cheese, 1 teaspoon of the parsley, and the garlic. Mix well. Sprinkle an equal amount of the stuffing mixture over each piece of meat. Starting from a narrow end, roll up tightly and secure with two crisscrossed toothpicks.

Heat the olive oil in the pressure cooker over medium-high heat. Add the onion and sauté 1 minute. Add the pork bundles in small batches and brown on all sides. Remove to a dish and set aside. When all the bundles have been browned, return them to the pressure cooker with any collected juices and sprinkle with the salt and black pepper. Pour in the wine and stir well. Raise the heat to high.

Position the lid and lock in place. Bring to high pressure. Adjust the heat to stabilize the pressure and cook 10 minutes. Remove from the heat and lower the pressure using the cold-water-release method. Open the pressure cooker. Remove the *involtini* from the pressure cooker and place on a serving dish. Pour the sauce over the *involtini* and sprinkle with the remaining parsley before serving.

4 SERVINGS

APPROXIMATE NUTRITIONAL ANALYSIS PER SERVING
606 calories, 41g protein, 26g carbohydrates, 35g fat, 168mg cholesterol, 669mg sodium

PORK SIMMERED IN MILK AND HERBS
Lomo de Cerdo con Leche

◆ *Arrosto di Maiale al Latte, Italy*

Roasting in milk is a popular Spanish and Italian method for preparing pork. The milk initially tenderizes the meat as it cooks. As it evaporates, the milk thickens and combines with the natural juices of the meat, creating a delicious sauce. Quickly stirring as the sauce reduces and thickens prevents the sauce from separating.

3 tablespoons olive oil	1/2 teaspoon dried rosemary
1 1/2 pounds tenderloin of pork, trimmed of all visible fat and cut into 1 1/2-inch cubes	1 1/2 teaspoons salt
	1/8 teaspoon freshly ground black pepper
1 cup milk	1 tablespoon minced parsley
2 cloves garlic, peeled and minced	

Heat the olive oil in the pressure cooker over high heat. Add the pork and brown on all sides. Add the milk, garlic, rosemary, salt, and black pepper. Position the lid and lock in place. Bring to high pressure. Adjust the heat to stabilize the pressure and cook 20 minutes. Remove from the heat and lower the pressure using the cold-water-release method. Open the pressure cooker. Remove the pork with a slotted spoon and place on a plate. Cover and keep warm.

Place the pressure cooker on the burner uncovered. Stirring frequently, reduce the sauce over high heat until almost completely reduced. Taste and adjust for salt and pepper. Sprinkle with parsley before serving.

4 SERVINGS

APPROXIMATE NUTRITIONAL ANALYSIS PER SERVING
394 calories, 39g protein, 4g carbohydrates, 24g fat, 110mg cholesterol, 895mg sodium

LAMB AND CHICKPEA RAGOUT

MOROCCAN-INSPIRED

Moroccan cooking is characterized by fragrant, thick stews flavored with exotic spices. Meat dishes prepared with lamb and goat are characteristic of this country of nomadic herders, as in the following Moroccan-inspired recipe for lamb and chickpea ragout.

3 tablespoons olive oil
2 pounds boneless lamb shoulder, trimmed of all visible fat and cut into 1½-inch cubes
2 large onions, finely chopped
¼ cup dry white wine
28-ounce can plum tomatoes, drained, seeded, and chopped
½ cup Rich Beef Stock (page 48), or canned beef broth
½ teaspoon ground cinnamon
½ teaspoon crushed saffron threads

¼ teaspoon ground ginger
1 teaspoon salt
⅛ teaspoon freshly ground black pepper
1½ cups cooked chickpeas (page 63) or a 19-ounce can, drained and rinsed under cold water
¼ cup golden raisins (optional)
2 tablespoons finely chopped fresh cilantro for garnish

Heat the oil in the pressure cooker over high heat. Brown the lamb on all sides, in small batches. Remove the browned lamb and set aside. Lower the heat and add the onion. Sauté 4 to 5 minutes, or until soft. Stir frequently so that the onion does not brown. Return the lamb and any collected juices to the pressure cooker. Add the wine, tomatoes, beef stock, cinnamon, saffron, ginger, salt, and black pepper.

Position the lid and lock in place. Raise the heat to high and bring to high pressure. Adjust the heat to stabilize the pressure and cook 20 minutes. Remove from heat and lower pressure using the cold-water-release method. Open the pressure cooker and stir in the chickpeas and optional raisins. Taste and adjust for salt. Place the pressure cooker, uncovered, over low heat and simmer 10 minutes so that the raisins can plump and the flavors blend together. Garnish with cilantro before serving.

4 SERVINGS

APPROXIMATE NUTRITIONAL ANALYSIS PER SERVING

618 calories, 47g protein, 41g carbohydrates, 29g fat, 134mg cholesterol, 1068mg sodium

BRAISED LAMB
Tas Kebap

Both tomatoes and green peppers, brought to Europe over five hundred years ago by Spanish explorers, are recent introductions to Turkish cooking. They have been put to good use by Turkish cooks, appearing in many dishes like this braised lamb recipe.

3 tablespoons olive oil
1½ pounds boneless leg of lamb,
   trimmed of all visible fat, cut
   into 1-inch cubes
1 large onion, finely chopped
1 medium-sized green pepper, cut
   in half, cored, seeded, and finely
   chopped

1 cup canned crushed tomatoes
¼ cup water
¼ teaspoon ground allspice
1 teaspoon salt
¼ teaspoon freshly ground black
   pepper
2 tablespoons minced parsley

Heat the olive oil in the pressure cooker over high heat. Brown the lamb in two batches on all sides. Remove and set aside. Reduce the heat to low and sauté the onion and green pepper 4 to 5 minutes, or until soft. Stir frequently so the onion does not brown. Add the crushed tomatoes, water, allspice, salt, and black pepper. Sauté 2 minutes, stirring frequently. Add the browned lamb along with any collected juices. Stir well.

Position the lid and lock in place. Raise the heat to high and bring to high pressure. Adjust the heat to stabilize the pressure and cook 20 minutes. Remove from the heat and lower the pressure using the cold-water-release method. Open the pressure cooker. Taste and adjust for salt and pepper. Sprinkle with the minced parsley before serving.

4 SERVINGS

APPROXIMATE NUTRITIONAL ANALYSIS PER SERVING

356 calories, 36g protein, 7g carbohydrates, 20g fat, 109mg cholesterol, 717mg sodium

CHICKEN LIVER PÂTÉ
Pâté de Foie de Poulet

Fragrant with herbs and brandy, this rich, smooth pâté can be served with apéritifs or as a first course.

½ pound chicken livers, cleaned
   and deveined
1 medium onion, finely chopped
1 clove garlic, peeled and minced
4 strips bacon, coarsely chopped
4 slices day-old good-quality
   white bread, crusts removed,
   torn into small pieces
¼ teaspoon dried thyme
¼ teaspoon ground caraway seed
   (optional)

1 teaspoon salt
⅛ teaspoon freshly ground black
   pepper
1 large egg, lightly beaten
2 tablespoons brandy
Butter for greasing
1 bay leaf
1 cup water

Place the chicken livers, onion, garlic, bacon, and bread in the bowl of a food processor. Process using the pulse switch just until smooth. Add the thyme, ground caraway seeds, salt, black pepper, egg, and brandy. Process 30 seconds, or until well blended.

Butter a 2-cup deep ovenproof baking dish that fits in the pressure cooker. Spoon the pâté mixture into the dish. Place the bay leaf on top, pressing down slightly. Wrap the dish in two sheets of aluminum foil and seal well.

Pour the water into the pressure cooker. Place the steamer basket on the trivet. Place the prepared dish with the pâté in the steamer basket. Position the lid and lock in place. Place over high heat and bring to high pressure. Adjust the heat to stabilize the pressure and cook 35 minutes. Remove from the heat and lower the pressure using the natural-release method. Open the pressure cooker and carefully remove the steamer basket. Remove the aluminum foil and let cool on a wire rack to room temperature before serving.

8 SERVINGS

APPROXIMATE NUTRITIONAL ANALYSIS PER SERVING

142 calories, 8g protein, 10g carbohydrates, 7g fat, 109mg cholesterol, 515mg sodium

TAGINE OF CHICKEN AND OLIVES
Meslalla

In traditional Algerian cuisine, *meslalla* would be slowly cooked. Pressure cookers, introduced by French colonizers, changed how many people cooked, but provided equally delicious results. While I was initially surprised to see that the recipe called for three cups of chopped onions, I was even more surprised to see how they ultimately thickened and flavored the sauce in which the chicken cooks.

1/4 cup olive oil
3 cups finely chopped onions
6 medium carrots, peeled and
    finely chopped
6 garlic cloves, peeled and minced
2 tablespoons flour
4 skinless, boneless chicken breast
    halves, cut into quarters
2 cups water

1 bay leaf
1 1/2 teaspoons salt
1/8 teaspoon freshly ground black
    pepper
1 (10-ounce) jar pitted Spanish
    Manzanilla olives, drained and
    rinsed well under cold water
1 (6-ounce) package couscous
2 tablespoons minced parsley

Heat the olive oil in the pressure cooker over medium-high heat. Add the onions and sauté 4 to 5 minutes, or until soft. Stir frequently so that the onions do not brown. Add the chopped carrots and garlic and cook 2 minutes, stirring frequently. Sprinkle with the flour and stir well. Add the remaining ingredients, except the olives, parsley, and couscous.

Position the lid and lock in place. Raise the heat to high and bring to high pressure. Adjust the heat to stabilize the pressure, and cook 12 minutes. Remove from the heat and lower the pressure using the cold-water-release method. Open the pressure cooker and add the olives. Replace the lid and lock in place. Bring to high pressure over high heat, adjusting the heat to stabilize the pressure. Cook 3 minutes. Remove from the heat and lower the pressure using the cold-water-release method. Open the pressure cooker. Taste and adjust for salt and pepper.

Meslalla is traditionally served with couscous, which is readily available at most supermarkets and specialty food stores. Follow the instructions on the couscous package for making 4 to 5 servings. Once the couscous is ready, stir in 1 cup of the sauce from the *meslalla*. Mound the moistened couscous on a serving platter and form a large well in the center. With a slotted spoon carefully remove the chicken breasts and olives from the pressure cooker and place them in the center of the well. Spoon some of the sauce over the chicken and olives to moisten. Spoon the remaining sauce over the couscous and sprinkle with the minced parsley.

4 SERVINGS

APPROXIMATE NUTRITIONAL ANALYSIS PER SERVING

422 calories, 19g protein, 37g carbohydrates, 23g fat, 37mg cholesterol, 1553mg sodium

BRAISED CHICKEN WITH ORZO

This wonderfully simple, one-pot Algerian dish is the perfect meal to prepare when time is short and everyone is hungry.

6 tablespoons olive oil
1 cup orzo (rice-shaped pasta)
1 pound skinless, boneless chicken
   thighs or breasts, cut into
   1½-inch chunks
3 cloves garlic, peeled and minced
1 large onion, finely chopped

1⅔ cups water
1 tablespoon tomato paste
2 bay leaves
1½ teaspoons salt
⅛ teaspoon freshly ground black
   pepper

Heat 2 tablespoons of the olive oil in the pressure cooker over medium-high heat. Add the orzo and sauté, stirring frequently, about 4 to 5 minutes, or until the orzo becomes light golden brown. Remove at once from the pressure cooker to a small bowl. Set aside.

Heat the remaining 4 tablespoons of olive oil in the pressure cooker over high heat. Add the chicken, garlic, and onion. Sauté over high heat 6 to 8 minutes, or just until the chicken starts to brown. Stir frequently so that the onion does not brown. Add the water, tomato paste, bay leaves, salt, and black pepper. Stir well.

Position the lid and lock in place. Raise the heat to high and bring to high pressure. Adjust the heat to stabilize the pressure and cook 6 minutes. Remove from the heat and lower the pressure using the cold-water-release method. Open the pressure cooker. Taste and adjust for salt and pepper.

Stir in the browned orzo. Position the lid and lock in place. Place over high heat and bring to high pressure. Adjust the heat to stabilize the pressure and cook 4 minutes. Remove from the heat and lower the pressure using the cold-water-release method. Open the pressure cooker. If the orzo is not tender, simmer, uncovered, 2 to 3 minutes.

4 SERVINGS

APPROXIMATE NUTRITIONAL ANALYSIS PER SERVING

447 calories, 28g protein, 22g carbohydrates, 27g fat, 66mg cholesterol, 1426mg sodium

BRAISED FARMHOUSE CHICKEN
Pollo en Salsa

When laying hens are past their prime, they wind up in the stewpot. This remarkably easy recipe is a popular dish from Alhama de Granada, my wife's hometown in Spain. As the chicken braises, the cooking liquid combines with the natural juices of the chicken to produce a flavorful, rich sauce, which is traditionally served over matchstick-thin potatoes fried with whole, unpeeled cloves of garlic.

2 split chicken breasts with bone, about 2 pounds	8 cloves garlic, unpeeled
1/2 cup water	1 teaspoon paprika
1/2 cup dry white wine	2 teaspoons salt
1/2 cup olive oil	1 tablespoon whole black peppercorns
1 bay leaf	4 threads saffron, optional

Remove and discard the skin and all the visible fat from the chicken. Cut the breast halves into two or three pieces, cutting straight through the bone. Place the chicken in the pressure cooker. Add the remaining ingredients and stir to blend.

Position the lid and lock in place. Place over high heat and bring to high pressure. Adjust the heat to stabilize the pressure, and cook 15 minutes. Remove from the heat and lower the pressure using the cold-water-release method. Open the pressure cooker.

Place the pressure cooker, uncovered, on the burner over high heat and reduce the sauce by half. Stir periodically so that the chicken does not stick. Taste and adjust for salt.

If serving with fried potatoes, place the potatoes on a large serving platter. Lay the chicken pieces on top and spoon the sauce over.

4 SERVINGS

APPROXIMATE NUTRITIONAL ANALYSIS PER SERVING

371 calories, 16g protein, 3g carbohydrates, 18g fat, 41mg cholesterol, 1104mg sodium

PRESSURE COOKER "ROAST" CHICKEN GENOVESE-STYLE
Pollo alla Genovese

One of my favorite foods to prepare for a day at the beach or the mountains is roast chicken flavored with fresh herbs from my garden. Not having an air-conditioned kitchen, however, I try to avoid using the oven whenever possible in the summer. Fortunately, I stumbled upon this recipe years ago and was able to adapt it to the pressure cooker with excellent results.

One 2- to 2½-pound whole chicken, small enough to fit in the pressure cooker
½ teaspoon salt
⅛ teaspoon freshly ground black pepper
2 tablespoons chopped fresh parsley

4 sprigs fresh rosemary leaves, minced, or 1 teaspoon dried
4 cloves garlic, peeled and crushed
2 tablespoons flour
3 tablespoons olive oil
1 cup Rich Chicken Stock (page 47), or canned chicken broth

Remove all visible fat from chicken and rinse under cold water. Pat dry with paper towels. In a small bowl, combine the salt, black pepper, and half the parsley and rosemary. Rub the inside cavity of the chicken with this mixture. Place two of the garlic cloves in the cavity. Tie the legs together with string and tuck the wings back and under. Lightly dust the trussed chicken with the flour.

Heat the olive oil in the pressure cooker over high heat. Add the chicken and let brown to a light golden color on all sides, turning occasionally. Add the remaining parsley, rosemary, and garlic, along with the stock.

Position the lid and lock in place. Bring to high pressure. Adjust the heat to stabilize the pressure and cook 25 minutes. Remove from the heat and let the pressure release naturally. Open the pressure cooker. The chicken is done if the juices run clear when the leg is pricked with a fork. If the juice is pink, reposition the lid on the pressure cooker and lock in place. Cook an additional 3 to 5 minutes.

Remove the cooked chicken to a large serving platter and cover with foil. Place the pressure cooker back on the burner over high heat, uncovered, and bring the sauce to a boil. Reduce by half. Taste and adjust for salt. Cut the chicken into pieces and slice the breast meat from the bone. Pour the sauce through a strainer. Spoon the sauce over the cut-up chicken.

4 SERVINGS

APPROXIMATE NUTRITIONAL ANALYSIS PER SERVING

456 calories, 41g protein, 5g carbohydrates, 29g fat, 119mg cholesterol, 856mg sodium

CHICKEN STEWED IN TOMATO SAUCE
Pollo con Tomate Frito

This recipe is usually prepared in late summer, when tomatoes are at their best, after growing and ripening for weeks in the intense Spanish sun. The traditional accompaniment to this dish is a simple green salad and lots of crusty bread to sop up the tomato sauce—which, in my opinion, is the best part.

2 split chicken breasts with bone, about 2 pounds	5 cups thick tomato puree
¼ cup olive oil	3 teaspoons salt
2 large onions, finely chopped	⅛ teaspoon freshly ground black pepper

Remove and discard the skin and all the visible fat from the chicken. Cut the breast halves into three or four pieces, cutting straight through the bone. Heat the olive oil in the pressure cooker over high heat. Add the chicken a few pieces at a time and brown evenly on all sides. Remove and set aside. Add the onions and sauté over low heat 4 to 5 minutes, or until soft. Stir frequently so that the onions do not brown. Return the chicken to the pressure cooker along with any collected juices. Add the tomato puree, salt, and black pepper. Stir well.

Position the lid and lock in place. Bring to high pressure. Adjust the heat to stabilize the pressure and cook 25 minutes. Remove from the heat and lower the pressure using the cold-water-release method. Open the pressure cooker. Taste and adjust for salt and pepper.

4 SERVINGS

APPROXIMATE NUTRITIONAL ANALYSIS PER SERVING

539 calories, 45g protein, 38g carbohydrates, 25g fat, 107mg cholesterol, 2936mg sodium

CHICKEN WITH YOGURT AND BEER
Guisado de Pollo al Yogurt

While studying in Spain, I was our apartment's designated cook. I was always looking for new pressure-cooker recipes that were economical, filling, and nutritious. The following recipe was one of our favorites. The dish is simple to make, and the addition of beer and yogurt makes for a delicious sauce that also tenderizes the chicken.

2 chicken breasts, split, about
  2 pounds
3 tablespoons olive oil
1 large onion, cut in half and
  thinly sliced
1 cup plain yogurt

1/2 cup beer
1/2 teaspoon paprika
1/2 teaspoon oregano
1 1/2 teaspoons salt
1/8 teaspoon freshly ground black
  pepper

Remove and discard the skin and all the visible fat from the chicken. Cut the breast halves into three or four small pieces, cutting straight through the bone. Heat the olive oil in the pressure cooker over high heat. Add the chicken a few pieces at a time and brown evenly on all sides. Remove and set aside. Add the onion and sauté over low heat, 4 to 5 minutes, or until soft. Stir frequently so that the onion does not brown. Add the chicken along with any collected juices to the pressure cooker. Add the remaining ingredients and stir well.

Position the lid and lock in place. Raise the heat to high and bring to high pressure. Adjust the heat to stabilize the pressure and cook 15 minutes. Remove from heat and lower pressure using the cold-water-release method. Open the pressure cooker.

Place the pressure cooker, uncovered, on the burner over high heat and reduce the sauce by half. Stir periodically so that the chicken does not stick. Taste and adjust for salt and pepper.

4 SERVINGS

APPROXIMATE NUTRITIONAL ANALYSIS PER SERVING

415 calories, 44g protein, 9g carbohydrates, 21g fat, 109mg cholesterol, 938mg sodium

FRUITS AND SWEETS

FRUITS

The following cooking times are provided as guidelines to be used in cooking fruits in the pressure cooker. Cooking times can vary depending on the ripeness, quality, and size of the piece of fruit being cooked; maximum and minimum cooking times are given in some instances. When uncertain how long to cook something, always start with the shortest cooking time, since you can always continue cooking for an additional couple of minutes until the desired texture is reached.

Since water and liquids boil more slowly at 2,000 feet above sea level, the cooking time and the amount of cooking liquid needed must be increased accordingly. Please refer to page 28 for additional information.

All cooking times listed begin once high or maximum pressure is reached.

APPROXIMATE COOKING TIMES

FRESH AND DRIED FRUIT	COOKING TIME	AMOUNT COOKING LIQUID
Apples, fresh, slices or chunks	2 to 3 minutes	½ cup
Apples, slices, dried	3 minutes	½ cup
Apricots, fresh, whole or halved	2 to 3 minutes	½ cup
Apricots, dried	4 minutes	¾ cup
Berries, fresh	0 minutes*	½ cup
Cherries, fresh	0 minutes*	½ cup
Peaches, fresh, halved	3 minutes	½ cup
Peaches, dried	4 to 5 minutes	¾ cup
Pears, fresh, halved	3 to 4 minutes	½ cup
Pears, dried	4 to 5 minutes	¾ cup
Plums, fresh	0 minutes*	½ cup
Prunes	4 to 5 minutes	¾ cup
Quince, fresh, quartered	5 minutes	¾ cup
Raisins	4 to 5 minutes	¾ cup

Bring to high pressure, remove from the heat, and lower the pressure immediately using the cold-water-release method.

SPAIN

- ◆ *Marmelada, Portugal*
- ◆ *Cotognata, Italy*
- ◆ *Kythonopasto, Greece*

If you have never discovered quince, you are in for a wonderful surprise. This hard, yellow fruit that looks like a cross between an apple and a pear has been enjoyed by the people of the Mediterranean countries for well over 4,000 years. If it is not available at your local supermarket, try farmers' markets in late autumn and winter.

Extremely fragrant when ripe, quince are very dry and astringent and must be cooked with substantial quantities of sugar. Quince are high in pectin and are most commonly used in the Mediterranean countries in making a solid jamlike sweet that is either eaten alone or with semifirm cheese.

Quince cheese can also be enjoyed with soft rolls for breakfast or at coffee time, as in Sicily. The Greeks store quince cheese in a sealed container with two or three dried bay leaves. They then sprinkle the tops of the quince-cheese slices with granulated sugar before serving it as a sweet.

2½ pounds quince (about 5 large quince), cored, quartered, and cut into chunks (do not peel)	½ cup freshly squeezed lemon juice 2¼ cups sugar

Place the quince and lemon juice in the pressure cooker. Position the lid and lock in place. Place over high heat and bring to high pressure. Adjust the heat to stabilize the pressure and cook 5 minutes. Remove from the heat and release the pressure using the cold-water-release method. Open the pressure cooker and remove the cooked quince to a food mill using a slotted spoon. Mill until only skin remains.

Discard any remaining cooking liquid in the pressure cooker. Place the pureed quince and the sugar in the pressure cooker and stir well to blend. Over medium heat, bring the quince mixture to a boil. Lower the heat to a simmer and continue cooking, stirring constantly, until the mixture thickens to an oatmeal-like consistency and begins to come away from the sides of the pot. This can take anywhere from 20 to 25 minutes, depending on the moisture content and acidity of the quince. The quince mixture will also darken to a deep golden to reddish-brown, depending on the variety of quince used. The mixture has finished cooking when a spoonful turned upside down does not fall off the spoon.

Line a 1-quart loaf pan with a sheet of waxed paper. Pour the cooked quince mixture into the pan and spread evenly with a spatula. Set aside, uncovered. Let set at least 3 hours or overnight in a dry location.

The quince cheese is ready to be cut when it has solidified. Remove from the pan by turning upside down. Cut into thin slices and serve as they do in Spain and Portugal with a piece of semifirm sheep's-milk cheese like Spanish manchego or Italian fiore de Sardegna (slice the cheese into $1/8$-inch-thick slices and place a piece of quince cheese on top). You will find the contrast between the saltiness of the cheese and the tart sweetness of the quince to be delicious and interesting.

ABOUT **40** SLICES

APPROXIMATE NUTRITIONAL ANALYSIS PER SLICE

54 calories, 0g protein, 14g carbohydrates, 0g fat, 0mg cholesterol, 1mg sodium

RICE PUDDING
Arroz con Leche

◆ *Arroz Doce, Portugal*

Without a doubt, this is comfort food, Mediterranean-style. Slightly different from other versions of rice pudding, this recipe only contains rice and milk as the main two ingredients, with sugar, cinnamon, and lemon peel added for flavor. It is usually eaten warm and has more liquid than traditional rice pudding. It closely resembles a sweet version of risotto, rather than the egg-based rice pudding we are familiar with.

$^1/_2$ cup Italian arborio or other
   short-grain rice
$2^1/_2$ cups milk
$^1/_4$ cup sugar

1 pinch salt
1 3-inch cinnamon stick
1-inch slice of lemon peel

Rinse the rice in a colander under cold water. Place all the ingredients in the pressure cooker and stir to mix. Position the lid and lock in place. Place over high heat and bring to high pressure. Adjust the heat to stabilize the pressure and cook 25 minutes. Remove from the heat and lower the pressure using the natural-release method. Once the pressure has dropped, open the pressure cooker. Remove and discard the cinnamon stick and lemon peel. Spoon the rice into a serving bowl and cover with plastic wrap until ready to serve so a thick layer does not form on top. Serve warm.

4 SERVINGS

APPROXIMATE NUTRITIONAL ANALYSIS PER SERVING

207 calories, 6g protein, 34g carbohydrates, 5g fat, 21mg cholesterol, 75mg sodium

MEDITERRANEAN ACCOMPANIMENTS

The following are a few suggested salads to accompany many of the entrée recipes in this book. As you will see, the types of salad enjoyed in the Mediterranean countries vary distinctly from what is familiar to us—they are drawn from the vast variety of sun-ripened fruits and vegetables available in the region.

Orange Salad
Ensalada de Naranja

◆ *Insalata di Arance, Italy*

This refreshing orange salad was the winter standard in parts of Spain and Italy when seasonal salad fixings like lettuce and tomatoes were not available during the long days of winter. Even though that has changed, salads made with oranges and sweet onions are still popular when a splash of color and a refreshing alternative to salad greens are desired.

4 large eating oranges, peeled,
   white pith removed, sliced into
   ¼-inch rounds
1 small red onion, sliced into very
   thin rings and separated

Large pinch of sugar
6 tablespoons extra-virgin olive oil
¼ cup brine-cured black olives,
   patted dry with paper toweling

Lay the orange slices on a large serving dish. Cover with the sliced onion rings. Sprinkle the sugar over the oranges and onion. Drizzle with the olive oil and garnish with the olives. Let sit 30 minutes before serving to allow the flavors to blend.

4 SERVINGS

APPROXIMATE NUTRITIONAL ANALYSIS PER SERVING

230 calories, 2g protein, 24g carbohydrates, 21g fat, 0mg cholesterol, 74mg sodium

GREEN OLIVE SALAD
Olive Verde Condite

This pungent salad was usually prepared by farmers' wives using the olives grown on their own ancient olive trees. As they are extremely bitter, olives cannot be eaten straight from the tree. To make them palatable, they were usually crushed to split the flesh and then soaked in large vats of water that was changed daily as the natural acidity of the olives leached out. After about 45 to 60 days, the olives were usually cured enough to be preserved in large brine-filled vats. They were eaten plain or combined with other ingredients to make salads such as the one that follows.

½ cup extra-virgin olive oil
2 tablespoons white-wine vinegar
1 clove garlic, peeled and minced
2 tablespoons dried oregano
⅛ teaspoon crushed hot red
  pepper flakes (optional)

16 ounces brine-cured, large green
  olives, rinsed under water
1 small red onion, cut in half and
  sliced thin
2 stalks celery, coarsely chopped,
  including leaves

Combine the olive oil, vinegar, garlic, and oregano and the hot red pepper, if using, in a medium-sized serving bowl. Add the olives, onion, and celery. Stir well. Let sit 30 minutes before serving to allow the flavors to blend.

6 SERVINGS

APPROXIMATE NUTRITIONAL ANALYSIS PER SERVING

260 calories, 1g protein, 4g carbohydrates, 28g fat, 0mg cholesterol, 1823mg sodium

TOMATO AND FRESH MOZZARELLA SALAD
Insalata Caprese

ITALY

The success of this salad depends on the quality and freshness of the ingredients. Do not even attempt to makes this salad unless you can obtain vine-ripened tomatoes, fresh mozzarella, and fresh basil leaves. Without them, the results will be dismal. Be sure to have lots of crusty bread on hand to sop up the delicious juices.

4 firm, vine-ripened tomatoes, thinly sliced
1 teaspoon salt
1/2 pound fresh mozzarella cheese, thinly sliced

1 dozen fresh basil leaves
1/8 teaspoon freshly ground black pepper
6 tablespoons extra-virgin olive oil

Layer the tomatoes on a large serving dish. Sprinkle with the salt. Insert the mozzarella slices between the tomatoes, overlapping slightly. Sprinkle with the basil and black pepper. Drizzle with the olive oil. Let sit 30 minutes before serving to allow the flavors to blend.

4 SERVINGS

APPROXIMATE NUTRITIONAL ANALYSIS PER SERVING

388 calories, 13g protein, 7g carbohydrates, 35g fat, 41mg cholesterol, 908mg sodium

TOMATO, PEPPER, CUCUMBER, AND ONION SALAD
Pipirana

SPAIN

My wife has many memories of summers spent on her family's farm in Spain, especially of the August harvest, when scores of day laborers would converge to handpick the chickpeas and other legumes her father had planted in the spring. For breakfast, the workers were served platters of potatoes and peppers sautéed in locally pressed extra-virgin olive oil, along with bowls of *pipirana*, a chopped salad of Mediterranean vegetables tossed with olive oil and strong homemade vinegar. A plate of *pipirana*, served family-style, is still how the afternoon meal begins in many Spanish households during the hot days of summer.

2 large vipe-ripened tomatoes, cored and cut into ½-inch chunks

1 large green cubanelle pepper, cut in half, cored, seeded, and cut into ¼-inch dice

2 Kirby cucumbers, peeled and cut into ¼-inch dice

1 medium onion, coarsely chopped

¼ cup extra-virgin olive oil

2 tablespoons white-wine vinegar

1 teaspoon salt

Pinch freshly ground black pepper

Mix the vegetables together in a large serving bowl. Add the olive oil, vinegar, salt, and black pepper. Toss well. Taste and adjust for salt.

4 SERVINGS

APPROXIMATE NUTRITIONAL ANALYSIS PER SERVING

170 calories, 2g protein, 11g carbohydrates, 14g fat, 0mg cholesterol, 543mg sodium

YOGURT AND CUCUMBER SALAD
Talattaouri

This refreshing cucumber salad pairs perfectly with lamb dishes like Moroccan Lamb and Chickpea Ragout (page 165) and Turkish Braised Lamb (page 166).

4 Kirby cucumbers, peeled, cut into quarters, and thinly sliced
2 teaspoons salt
1½ cups plain yogurt
2 cloves garlic, peeled and crushed
2 teaspoons dried mint
2 tablespoons extra-virgin olive oil

Place the cucumbers in a colander over a bowl. Sprinkle with salt and let sit 1 hour, to allow the cucumbers to drain.

In a medium-sized mixing bowl, blend together the yogurt, garlic, mint, and olive oil. Add the drained cucumbers. Stir well.

4 SERVINGS

APPROXIMATE NUTRITIONAL ANALYSIS PER SERVING

152 calories, 8g protein, 16g carbohydrates, 7g fat, 2mg cholesterol, 1142mg sodium

SUGGESTED MENUS

◆ ◆ ◆

SPANISH TAPAS PARTY

for 8

Warm Shrimp and Bean Salad, **66**
Braised Artichokes, **95**
"Spanish" Russian Salad, **114**
Mussels à la Cataplana, **131**

Meatballs with Peas, **152**
Quince Cheese, **179**
Spanish manchego cheese
Green Olive Salad, **185**

◆ ◆ ◆

ITALIAN DINNER

for 4

Venetian-Style Artichokes, **97**
Pressure Cooker "Roast" Chicken
   Genovese-Style, **172**

Potato Pie, **116**
Twice-Cooked String Beans, **120**

◆ ◆ ◆

FRENCH COUNTRY SUPPER

for 4

Chicken Liver Pâté, **167**
Beef Stew from Provence, **143**

Egg noodles
Mixed green salad

◆ ◆ ◆

ITALIAN TRATTORIA LUNCH

for 4

Sweet-and-Sour Sicilian Eggplant, **107**
Stuffed Pork Bundles, **163**

Roman-Style Pressure-Roasted Potatoes, **112**
Tomato and Fresh Mozzarella Salad, **186**

◆ ◆ ◆

SPANISH HOME-STYLE SUPPER

for 4

Loin of Pork with Bitter Orange Sauce, **162**   Orange Salad, **184**
String Beans and Potatoes, **118**   Rice Pudding, **181**

◆ ◆ ◆

WINTER DINNER PARTY

for 4

Roman Egg-Drop Soup, **52**   Mashed potatoes
Veal Stew with Red Peppers, **154**   Tossed green salad

◆ ◆ ◆

SPECIAL CELEBRATION DINNER

for 4

Risotto with Saffron, **87**   Braised Veal Shanks, **155**
String Bean Salad with Potatoes, **119**

◆ ◆ ◆

LATE-NIGHT IMPROMPTU SUPPER

for 4

Carrot Salad, **103**   Braised Chicken with Orzo, **170**

◆ ◆ ◆

TURKISH SUPPER

for 4

Braised Lamb, **166**   Basic Rice Pilaf, **89**   Yogurt and Cucumber Salad, **188**

◆ ◆ ◆

VEGETARIAN DINNER

for 4

Chickpea Spread, **76**   Vegetable Stew with Couscous, **122**
Tomato, Pepper, Cucumber, and Onion Salad, **187**

TROUBLESHOOTING

For best results in using your pressure cooker, be sure to read and refer to the Introduction, especially pages 20 to 32, and all the printed and instructional materials provided by the pressure-cooker manufacturer.

PROBLEM:

No pressure buildup.

REASON:

1. Not enough cooking liquid.
2. The pressure cooker was not properly closed.
3. The pressure cooker was not heated over high enough heat.
4. The pressure-regulator valve is dirty and/or obstructed.
5. The rubber sealing gasket or ring is:
   a. not in place
   b. improperly positioned
   c. dirty
   d. worn
6. The pressure cooker was damaged and the safety valve has activated or is blocked, inhibiting pressure buildup.

SOLUTION:

1. Always use a sufficient amount of cooking liquid for the type of food being prepared and the length of cooking. Consult the pressure-cooker recipe you are following, or the cooking guidelines found in the beginning of each chapter.
2. Follow the instructions on page 26 on how to close the pressure cooker properly or refer to the instructional materials provided by the manufacturer so that a tight seal is created allowing for adequate pressure buildup.
3. Always heat the closed pressure cooker over high heat until high pressure has been reached.

4. The pressure-regulator valve can become dirty when cooking. Clean the valve after each use as explained on pages 25 and 30 and in the instructional materials provided by the manufacturer.

5. a. Before using the pressure cooker, always check to make sure that the rubber sealing gasket or ring is inserted.

   b. Always check to see that the rubber sealing gasket or ring is *properly* inserted before using the pressure cooker each time.

   c. The rubber sealing gasket or ring should be removed from the lid and washed after each use. Refer to pages 22 and 30 or the instructional materials provided by the manufacturer for care and cleaning information.

   d. After continued use, the rubber sealing gasket or ring will begin to wear or dry out. It should be replaced at least once a year, or more often if the pressure cooker is used frequently.

6. In the event that the pressure cooker or any of its safety valves are damaged, the safety valves will kick in and pressure buildup will be inhibited. In the event that this should happen, contact the manufacturer's customer service department for after-sales repair assistance.

PROBLEM:

1. Small drops of water condensation collect on the lid and/or a popping sound is heard.

REASON:

1. It is normal that some drops of condensed water appear on the lid while you are cooking, and it is not unusual to hear an audible popping sound.

PROBLEM:

2. A large, steady stream of steam is escaping from pressure-regulator valve with or without drops of condensation.

REASON:

2. a. The burner heat is too high.

   b. The pressure-regulator valve is dirty.

   c. The pressure-regulator valve may be malfunctioning.

SOLUTION:

1. Normal operation.

2. a. Lower the burner heat so that the pressure-regulator valve registers the desired level of pressure. For building and maintaining pressure, refer to page 27 or consult the manufacturer's instructional materials.

   b. Clean the pressure-regulator valve after each use, as explained on pages 25 and 30, or consult the manufacturer's instructional materials.

   c. The pressure-regulator valve must be replaced. Contact the manufacturer's customer service department for repair information.

PROBLEM:

Steam is escaping from around the edge of the lid.

REASON:

1. The pressure cooker is too full.
2. The pressure cooker was not closed properly.
3. The rubber gasket is:
   a. not in place.
   b. dirty.
   c. worn.

SOLUTION:

1. Never fill the pressure cooker more than two-thirds full.
2. Make sure the pressure cooker is properly closed, so that a tight seal is created. Refer to page 26, or consult the manufacturer's instructional materials.
3. a. Always check to see that the rubber sealing gasket or ring is properly positioned before using the pressure cooker.
   b. Always remove and wash the rubber sealing gasket or ring after using the pressure cooker. Refer to pages 22 and 30 or the manufacturer's instructional materials. Be sure to dry well and reinsert under the inside rim of the lid before putting away.
   c. After continued use, the rubber sealing gasket or ring will begin to wear or dry out. It should be replaced at least once a year or more often if the pressure cooker is used frequently.

PROBLEM:

The pressure cooker cannot be opened after cooking.

REASON:

1. There is still built-up pressure in the pressure cooker.
2. In the event that the natural-release period was long, a slight vacuum may have developed.
3. The safety valve has activated.

SOLUTION:

1. Use the cold-water-release method to release any remaining pressure. Try opening again.
2. Heat the pressure cooker over high heat just until steam begins to come out of the pressure-regulator valve. Using the cold-water-release method, release the pressure and try to open.
3. Consult the manufacturer's instructional materials.

PROBLEM:

Foods are undercooked.

REASON:

1. Cooking time was too short.
2. Cold-water-release method was incorrectly used to release pressure.

SOLUTION:

1. Always consult the cooking times provided in the recipe or the cooking guide-lines at the beginning of each chapter. If food is still undercooked, extend the cooking time by about 1 to 2 minutes, and cook under pressure until the desired texture is achieved.
2. When called for in the recipe, use the slower, natural-release method as explained on page 29, so that the food has the benefit of additional cooking time as the pressure drops.

PROBLEM:

Food is overcooked.

REASON:

1. Cooking is too long.
2. Natural-release method was incorrectly used.

SOLUTION:

1. Always consult the cooking times provided in the recipe or the cooking guide-lines at the beginning of each chapter. If the food is still overcooked, next time shorten the cooking time by at least 1 to 2 minutes.
2. Use the cold-water-release method, as explained on page 29 so that the pressure drops immediately.

PRESSURE-COOKER MANUFACTURERS

The following pressure-cooker manufacturers kindly provided me with samples and/or product information used in developing this cookbook. For your convenience, I have provided the manufacturers' customer-service phone numbers in the event that you should have any questions regarding the use of your pressure cooker.

Cuisinart
800-726-0190

Kuhn-Rikon
800-662-5882

Mirro
800-518-6245

Decor
800-923-8700

Lagostina
800-363-6247

Presto
800-877-0441

Fagor
800-207-0806

Maantra
800-378-0888

Sitram
800-969-2518

Innova
800-767-5160

Magafesa
800-923-8700

T-Fal
800-395-8325

INDEX